Film

Social Fictions Series

The titles published in this series are listed at *brill.com/soci*

Film

By

Patricia Leavy

BRILL

SENSE

LEIDEN | BOSTON

All chapters in this book have undergone peer review.

The Library of Congress Cataloging-in-Publication Data is available online at
http://catalog.loc.gov

ISSN 2542-8799
ISBN 978-90-04-41401-3 (paperback)
ISBN 978-90-04-41402-0 (hardback)
ISBN 978-90-04-41403-7 (e-book)

This book is printed on acid-free paper and produced in a sustainable manner.

PRAISE FOR *FILM*

"Placing women's experiences in the forefront, *Film* tells a powerful story of three women who overcome obstacles in pursuit of their dreams. With a subtext of sexual harassment and inequality especially relevant in the #MeToo era, this timely novel illustrates the cultural context in which girls and women live their lives. An engaging read, *Film* is sure to stimulate reflection, both personally and more broadly in book clubs and courses on media and gender."
– Jean Kilbourne, Ed.D., author, feminist activist, and creator of the *Killing Us Softly: Advertising's Image of Women* film series

"This novel is written for anyone who has ever confronted the shadow side of their life to find the courage to light their own fire. *Film* provides inspirational fuel for forging the life, work, and art we need by watching Tash, Lu, and Monroe realize their own passions in a sexist culture. *Film* is a feminist fist bump and a gorgeous visual of what women helping women and being your own muse looks like on the big screen of our lives."
– Sandra L. Faulkner, Ph.D., Bowling Green State University, and author of *Poetic Inquiry: Craft, Method, and Practice*

"Once you pick up this book, you won't be able to put it down. Like Leavy's previous novels, *Film* shows us how beautiful our lives can be when we embrace possibilities. It's a powerful commentary on living your best life, one that will leave you inspired."
– Jessica Smartt Gullion, Ph.D., Texas Woman's University, and author of *Writing Ethnography*

"*Film* is a tour de force! This timely novel speaks powerfully to the challenges many women face. Can we be in meaningful and fulfilling relationships and still hold true to ourselves and fulfill our own 'big' dreams? *Film* transported me to Los Angeles, the place to be for creatives who want to succeed. It is the apex of pop culture, and for the characters in *Film*, pop culture is not trivial: it is part of who they are in their hearts and souls. They want to both be 'in' it and move it to new places. Leavy's talent for combining the fun and glitz of LA with profound cultural insights is unmatched. *Film* is a page-turner, but also dives deep beneath the surface. This is Leavy's greatest skill, along with her ability to write characters with whom we empathize. The people in this novel bring with them their familial histories, their #MeToo experiences, and their desire to make it in La La Land. They have 'big' dreams, and we root for them as they overcome their obstacles and discover what really matters. I love how the characters in the novel are not in lockstep with each other, but can fully support each other's dreams and help each other overcome their past failures and pains. Reading about these women makes me feel good, as if my contribution to the Women's Movement has helped create their lives. I couldn't put this book down. *Film* takes you inside yourself, and outside, too. It inspires a belief in *possibility.* Bravo! I love all of Patricia Leavy's novels, but *Film* is absolutely gorgeous."
– Laurel Richardson, Ph.D., The Ohio State University, and author of *Lone Twin*

"An engaging reminder of the struggles that come and go in the course of a life, *Film* captures the experiences of multiple women at transformational times in their lives and demonstrates the importance of persistence, creativity, and support for the achievement of one's dreams. Returning to the life of Tash Daniels, from Leavy's prior novels *Blue* and *Low-Fat Love*, the novel swims at a beautiful pace with an undercurrent of sexual and gender tension and conflict especially fitting for talking and teaching about our current social world."
– J. E. Sumerau, Ph.D., The University of Tampa, and author of *Palmetto Rose*

"*Film* is a novel I had no idea I was waiting for until I started to read it. We are immersed in a world tailor-made for any audience, one which offers an insightful glimpse into life after college and those confusing years of our twenties. The concept of a 'big life' is returned to in the world of Tash, now a college graduate finding her way through the thorny world of deciding and accepting her future. At what point do we choose our 'big life' or learn to accept that 'big' means happiness and not wealth? When do we leave behind our unrealistic expectations of easily attained success and embrace our true passions, even if they are hard and don't immediately offer a path to material prosperity? How do we get in our own way? How do unaddressed past traumas leak into our present and prevent us from moving forward? There are so many elements that demonstrate Leavy's expertise in explicitly and implicitly drawing out the truths at the heart of humanity in today's world in ways we can all relate to, while creating a story that feels incredibly intimate. But Leavy's greatest talent is writing stories for varied audiences that can be read at multiple levels, from consuming them in an afternoon on the beach to doing a deep analysis in the classroom. I've used *Low-Fat Love* (2011) in class many times because it resonates with the students in ways general scholarly material cannot, feeling accessible and thus understandable. *Film* provides an even more nuanced look into a phase of life already murky in some imaginations, yet one we can recognize at whatever point of life's journey we are on. Leavy's diverse range of characters helps students see versions of themselves while developing empathy for the complexities of difference. It's also her bravest novel, dealing with issues sparked by the current #MeToo Movement, in a sensitive yet direct way that will resonate with any reader. Her characters help us all realize that we only really see shades of people, tips of icebergs that often hide deep wells of pain. I could write a thousand pages of reasons to consume this novel on a lazy afternoon, since once you start you won't be able to put it down. I could even write a long list of reasons to use this novel in your Contemporary History, Social Work, Communication, Film, Women's and Gender Studies, Sociology, and Capstone courses. In the end, you should just read it and judge for yourself. I promise you won't be disappointed."
– U. Melissa Anyiwo, Ph.D., Curry College, and editor of *Gender Warriors: Teaching Contemporary Urban Fantasy*

"*Film* is the final installment in a trilogy that begins with *Low-Fat Love* and continues with *Blue*. These three novels operate as research artworks as well as a suite of connected, yet stand-alone stories. *Film*, like the other books, is a love letter to popular culture, and in particular, illustrates how art may sustain us through life's challenges when those around us may not. This latest work has its own strong sense of self, whilst simultaneously being a novel about how we must maintain our own sense of authentic self, remaining true to our creative identities, practices, and aspirations. In this way, *Film* is a staging of desire, possibility, and sensitivity. As always, Patricia Leavy has gifted us a highly readable, enjoyable, and engaging public and (most importantly, in my view) accessible piece of scholarship. Her voice is palpable and inviting as she draws vivid and knowable, strong and complex characters, to whom many can relate in their struggles for success and desire. Leavy's refreshing and authentic dialogue and relatable plotting defy the complexity of the work and its subtexts about opportunity, creativity, and privilege, as well as feminism, equity, and sexuality. A proactive reader will note the theory in the work, will hear the research at its core. Some will read for the absolute entertainment value. This is arts-based research at its best: accessible and refreshing to read, yet layered and nuanced in its textures of scholarship. Patricia Leavy has delivered another title in her original and unique voice, yet again demonstrating her mettle as a masterful writer of fiction as research."
– **Alexandra Lasczik, Ph.D., Southern Cross University**

Also from Patricia Leavy

Privilege Through the Looking-Glass

Low-Fat Love Stories
By Patricia Leavy and Victoria Scotti

Blue

American Circumstance: Anniversary Edition

Low-Fat Love: Expanded Anniversary Edition

Gender & Pop Culture: A Text-Reader
Edited by Adrienne Trier-Bieniek and Patricia Leavy

For more information, visit the author's website
www.patricialeavy.com

To everyone who has stumbled while pursuing a dream
but found the courage to keep going,
and to those who have lent a helping hand

CONTENTS

CONTENTS

PREFACE

Film follows three women who moved to Los Angeles to pursue their dreams. Tash Daniels aspires to be a filmmaker. Her short film was rejected from festivals, she has a stack of rejected grant proposals, and she lost her internship at a studio when her boss sexually harassed her, forcing her to take a job as a personal shopper. Lu K is a hot deejay, slowly working her way up the club scene, but no one is doing her any favors. Fiercely independent, she's at a loss when she meets Paisley, a woman who captures her heart. Monroe Preston is the glamorous wife of a Hollywood studio head. As a teenager, she moved to LA in search of a "big" life, but now she wonders if reality measures up to fantasy. When a man in their circle finds sudden fame, each of these women is catapulted on a journey of self-discovery. Tash struggles with staying invested in art-making when she has nothing but rejections to show for her efforts. She begins to spiral into old habits and question her path and identity. Lu and Paisley may be the perfect couple, but the idea of a perfect connection bewilders Lu. She has always pushed uncomfortable thoughts out of her mind, but when she enters Paisley's world of close friends and family, Lu finally allows herself to remember her past. Monroe develops crippling insomnia as she begins to obsess over turning points in her youth and a painful revelation about her mother.

As the characters' stories unfold, each is forced to confront how her past has shaped her fears and to choose how she wants to live in the present. *Film* is a novel about the underside of dreams, the struggle to find internal strength, the power of art, and what it truly means to live a "big" life. Bathed in the glow of the silver screen, the characters in *Film* show us how the arts can reignite the light within. With a tribute to art and popular culture, set against the backdrop of Tinseltown, *Film* celebrates how the art we make and experience shapes our stories, scene by scene.

I decided to write *Film* the day I finished *Blue* (which I elaborate on in the afterword). However, I had to wait until I completed other projects. As it turned out, the timing was auspicious. Themes of sexual harassment and rape culture underscore the narrative. While those subjects were always intended to be part of this novel, even prior to the #MeToo movement and Time's Up initiative, these cultural shifts further propelled my writing.

The writing style employed in this novel is meant to accentuate central themes. For example, flashback scenes show the traumas the characters have faced in their pasts, including sexual harassment and assault. These flashbacks help illustrate how the characters have become who they presently are. I also wanted to explore sociologist Erving Goffman's notion of "front stage" (our public faces) and "back stage" (our private selves). Coupled with other techniques, including interior dialogue, these flashbacks allowed for a sociological analysis of "front" and "back" stage, thereby dismantling the appearance of who these characters are, and instead exploring what lurks behind the scenes and how the backstage impacts the public personas the characters develop. Language is also used in specific ways. Some words and phrases are repeated across scenes or across characters. For example, all the characters eat eggs (a symbol for emergence and rebirth), all are shown in the glow of film (a transformational element), and the word "edge" comes up repeatedly for each character (as each is on the edge of something, and likewise, each is searching for her own edge). The word "film" is also prominent, taking on different meanings in each of the character's lives.

From the day I began writing *Film*, it was special to me. I've never enjoyed writing something so much. I began to think of this novel as a lifeline during challenging social and political times and as a love letter to my younger self. This is the women-centered story I wish I had read years ago. At its core, this is a story about women supporting women, lighting our own fires, and harnessing the power of art to save us. My previous novels have open endings that explicitly defy norms. *Film* has my version of a happy ending, one that offers an alternative to what is typically portrayed in popular culture. I'm elated to share it and I hope it serves as solace and inspiration. Light your own fire.

Patricia Leavy

PART ONE

CHAPTER 1

Tash used her palm to wipe the steam off the bathroom mirror. *Damn the LA sun. Are my freckles actually getting bigger?* She began rubbing foundation on her face, followed by blush, highlighter, her signature black liquid eyeliner, and mascara. *My eyes look fierce*, she thought, staring at her reflection. *I wish I hadn't agreed to work for Monroe today. At least I can party tonight.* After curling the ends of her perfectly straightened, long hair, she headed to the bedroom to get dressed.

While rifling through her underwear drawer, she noticed her favorite Polaroid of her, Jason, and Penelope in their old New York apartment. *Jason was so funny with that old-school camera. I miss him. Both of them.* Never one to display her vulnerability, she tucked the photo safely back at the bottom of the drawer. From her closet, she selected black leggings, a light gray tunic with strategically placed cutouts, and black gladiator sandals. She got dressed and looked herself over, putting on small, gold hoop earrings. *Something's missing.* She surveyed her closet. *Aww, perfect. Haven't worn you in ages*, she thought as she snatched her favorite black fedora, bought that day on Macdougal Street in New York, when Aidan first said, "I love you." The hat always reminded her of that day. Running her fingers along the rim, she wondered why it had been so hard to say I love you in return. *I did love him*, she lamented, placing the hat on her head. She took a final glance in the mirror. *Now I'm ready.*

Grabbing her slouchy black leather bag, she searched for her sunglasses and car key. Finding neither, she scoured the dresser. *Shit. Where's the key? I hate that you can't get anywhere in LA without a car. Must be on the mail table.* As she approached the small table by the door, she spotted her sunglasses, car key, and latest rejection letter. She slipped the glasses on her head and stared at the folded paper. *Don't do it, Tash*, she warned herself, but it was too late. She picked up the letter and began reading. *Dear Ms. Daniels, We regret to inform you that you have not been chosen to receive our screen writing grant.*

With the highest submission rate we have ever received... blah, blah, blah. Same shit, different day. At least when these jerks reject me, they don't tell me everything that's wrong with my work, unlike those film festival scumbags. Whatever. She crumpled the letter, tossed it in the trash, and headed out.

***

"Stop honking, you assholes," Tash muttered. *Why does anyone think they can get anywhere quickly in this town? I hope Monroe isn't pissed if I'm late again. I still can't believe I came to LA and all I'm doing is this personal shopping crap. At least when I worked retail in New York I wasn't stuck in gridlock. Monroe's life is a trip though.* Tash remembered the day they met, over a year ago. She was rummaging through a post-holiday sale accessory table at a store on Rodeo Drive, searching for the perfect bangle bracelet. A striking woman with platinum hair, who Tash pegged for mid-forties although she looked much younger, came out of the dressing room wearing an ankle-length, ivory dress. The saleswoman scurried over.

"I'm just not sure it's flattering on me. What about the color?"

"It's very sophisticated," the saleswoman assured her.

Tash snorted.

The woman turned to her. "Excuse me, Miss. I don't want to bother you, but what do you think of this dress?"

"It's fine," Tash said, returning her attention to a seventy-five percent off jewelry bin.

"Please, I usually shop with friends or my assistant, but she recently quit to get married. I need an honest opinion. It's for a dinner party."

Tash dropped a handful of earrings and turned toward the woman. "That color is horrible on you. You have flawless skin; I'd actually kill for your complexion, but that dress washes you out. And you're swallowed up in fabric. It makes you look matronly and you're obviously hot, like, really hot."

The woman blushed. "It's an upscale event."

"Unless that's code for old lady event, you should show some skin, tastefully. Hang on, I'll find you something," Tash said.

"I'm a size…"

"Six, I know. I worked retail for a couple of years."

A moment later, Tash returned with a knee-length black crepe dress with three-quarter length flouncy silk sleeves. She held it out and said, "Before we waste any time, do you have good legs?"

"Well, uh…" the woman stammered.

"Veins or no veins? Just be honest," Tash said.

"No veins. I have nice legs."

Tash handed her the garment. Minutes later, she emerged from the dressing room, beaming.

The saleswoman ran over. "Oh, that looks great on you too. You could wear anything."

Tash rolled her eyes. "That's much better. You look ten years younger. And it's on sale," she said, smirking at the saleswoman. "Well, enjoy your party," she said, returning her attention to the sale table.

The woman extended her hand. "My name is Monroe Preston."

"Nice to meet you. I'm Tash, Tash Daniels."

They shook hands and Monroe said, "Please give the salesgirl whatever you were looking at. My treat."

Tash laughed. "That's okay."

"Please, I insist," Monroe said.

A little later, as they were checking out, Monroe handed her a small bag with the three gold bangles Tash selected.

"Thanks for the bling."

"My pleasure. It was wonderfully refreshing to have someone tell me the truth."

"I get that," Tash replied.

"You mentioned you've worked in retail?"

"Yeah, but I haven't done that in a while. I moved to LA to work in film, well, whatever, it's a long story. I had an internship at a film studio, but quit when my boss tried to feel me up. It was kind of a regular thing, but I finally had enough."

"That's awful. You couldn't report him?"

"Who would care? He was someone. I was no one."

"I understand how it works," Monroe said, wistfully. "What are you doing now?"

"You know those studio tours?"

Monroe nodded.

"I drive one of those trams. It's beyond awful, but it's all I could get. I'm really a filmmaker, though, and a writer. Aspiring, anyway. I have a short film that's almost done. I'll be submitting it to festivals and stuff."

"If you could use a flexible part-time job, I'd like to hire you as my personal shopper."

"Oh, I don't know."

"I'll pay you extremely well. More than you earn now."

Tash bit her lip and gave Monroe the once-over. "You know what? I'll do it. If I have to drive that tram one more day so tourists can take pictures on the *Friends* couch, I might explode."

"Splendid! Do you have time right now? I have a couple of hours before my Kabbalah class and I need shoes. We could stop for lunch. This calls for a champagne toast," Monroe said.

Tash smiled. "I'm in."

The two got along smashingly from that day forward. Monroe was never short on money; Tash was never short on candor.

***

Miraculously, Tash arrived at Monroe's estate on time. She was immediately buzzed through the security gates. Although she detested Beverly Hills, she thought the Spanish-style mansion set behind palm trees on a perfectly landscaped property would be an ideal film location. It was impossibly Los Angeles and reeked of throwback Hollywood glamour. Some days Monroe opened the door herself, looking like a movie star from the 1940s or '50s. Her resemblance to Marilyn Monroe was uncanny, and like her idol, Tash learned that she had changed her name to fit the big life she imagined for herself. On this day, Henry, the butler, let her in.

"Hey there, H," Tash said.

"Hello, Miss Daniels. Mrs. Preston is in her dressing room."

"Thanks," Tash said, flying up the grand staircase.

Tash walked right into Monroe's bedroom and through to her dressing room. Monroe, wearing a white silk robe, was seated on a pink leather ottoman, looking through a stack of shoeboxes.

"Oh, hi Tash. I'm glad you're here. I want to donate some of these to charity, but I'm not sure what to hold on to. And the clothes you ordered have arrived. Also, I have three events this weekend to prepare for."

For the next two hours, they sorted shoes and Monroe tried on outfits while Tash styled them with accessories. As Monroe had come to expect, Tash wasn't shy about assessing each look or admonishing a store for sending pieces Tash hadn't preapproved. When Monroe tried on a gray silk halter dress, Tash abruptly said, "Uh, no. Just no. You're not going to a party at the Playboy mansion." Monroe giggled. No one spoke to her that way and she adored Tash for it.

By the time they were done, Monroe had all her looks for the weekend selected, two garment bags full of items for Tash to return, and several shoeboxes designated for charity. When Monroe told her to take any of the shoes she liked, Tash selected a pair of black Prada heels. Monroe was half a size larger, but for shoes like that, Tash would stuff them with cotton balls to make them work.

"Okay, so I'll take these with me. I know you want to start planning the gifts you need for next month as well as the hostess gifts for your garden lunch. Would you like me to stop by on Monday?" Tash asked.

"I'm having a little something done on Monday. Can you come at lunchtime on Tuesday? I'll have the cook prepare something for us. You can bring your swimsuit if you want to take a dip before you leave."

"Sounds good. And whatever you're doing Monday, just remember: less is more."

Monroe smiled. "You're such a sweetheart," she said, hugging her.

On her way out, Tash turned and said, "Don't forget, Band-Aids on the back of your heels Saturday night. Those shoes aren't broken in."

"I'll remember. Thank you, Tash."

Tash winked and headed out, carrying the garment bags and her new shoes.

***

After spending hours in traffic to return Monroe's unwanted garments on opposite sides of LA, Tash stopped at home for a quick bite and to get ready for the night. Decked out in a t-shirt style, black sequin mini-dress and her new Prada heels, she headed out again. She noticed her neighbor Darrell going into his apartment. He was carrying canvases under his arm, the white cloth stark against his dark skin. She waved and he nodded in return. *Quiet dude*, she thought.

She arrived at the club at ten o'clock, after easily finding a parking space.

"Yo, T," a bouncer called as she bypassed the long line.

"Hey, Jimmie," she said as he unlatched the rope, letting her in.

She walked into the mammoth space, lit with blue lights. Electro house music was blaring and the whole room of beautiful people pulsed like an excited heartbeat. As she wiggled through the crowd on her way to the bar, Texas gently touched her arm, his shaggy, blonde hair brushing the front of her face. "Well hey there, Tash," he said in his southern drawl.

"Hey, Texas. I'm in desperate need of booze. Catch ya later, okay?"

"Sure thing," he said with a tilt of his chin.

He's sweet and I don't mind the flirt, but I'm so not in the mood tonight. She approached the bar and without a word, Leo handed her a tequila sunrise.

"You're the best bartender in LA," she said, taking the drink. She took a sip while scanning the room. Lu, her best friend in LA, spotted her and was already sauntering over. Tall with short blonde hair and dripping with it-girl charisma, Lu stood out in the crowd. Tonight, she was wearing black leather pants and an old Depeche Mode tank top that showed off her toned arms. Tash watched as every lesbian and bi woman in the place checked her out.

"Hey, baby," Tash said.

"Hey, babe. This place is on tonight," Lu said.

"You're lookin' good. Very butch-chic."

"You know it. I'm digging your vibe, very Liza Minnelli meets pole dancer."

"Good one, baby. Prowling for some poor girl to hook up with?" Tash mused.

"My own personal Jesus," Lu said with a laugh.

"You're a heartbreaker," Tash teased.

"Speaking of, your little southern admirer is here," Lu said, grabbing Tash's drink and taking a gulp.

"Oh yeah. He's already made his presence known."

Lu smiled.

"You working tonight?" Tash asked.

Lu nodded. "Yeah, I'll go take over for your boy so you can have some time. Give me another hit of that first."

Lu took another sip of Tash's drink and they both started walking toward the deejay platform.

"See ya later," Lu said.

Tash waved and looked up. With his headphones on and working his sound, Aidan had never been sexier. He looked straight at her, grinning from ear to ear.

She smiled and mouthed, "I love you."

CHAPTER 2

Lu's alarm sounded at eight o'clock in the morning. Too exhausted to open her eyes, she felt around for her phone and turned it off. *Damn. This schedule is killing me. I can't wait to sleep tomorrow. Better get my ass out of bed before I pass out again.* She slithered up to a sitting position and forced her eyes open, the crust in the corners acting like glue. She yawned, long and slow, and then shook her head, trying to wake up. *I'm cold*, she thought, grabbing a pullover hoodie off the floor and putting it on as she shuffled out of bed. "Damn!" she hollered, stubbing her toe on the laptop she left on the floor. She rose again, only to trip on a pile of clothes as she tried to make her way to the galley kitchen of her studio apartment. She set up the coffee pot, accidentally spilling some grounds on the counter, which she brushed into her hand and dumped into the coffee maker.

As the coffee brewed, she leaned on the counter and shut her eyes. The alarm rang again, startling her. "Fuck. I must have hit snooze," she grumbled. She noticed five unread texts: four from women she met the night before, each making sure she had their number, and one from Tash, promising to see her that night. She responded to Tash:

```
Thanks, babe. But dude, if you need
tonight w/your man, no worries.
```

When the coffee machine finally beeped, she filled a mug and her to-go tumbler. She placed the tumbler next to her sunglasses on her small, two-person table, so that she'd remember it. With the mug in hand, she headed to the bathroom, slurping the steaming coffee on the way. "Well, that's a look," she said upon seeing herself in the mirror, hair matted to one side and bags under her eyes. *Please let the hot water be working*, she prayed, flipping the shower on. *Fuck. It's ice cold again.*

***

Lu arrived at the juice bar to find the typical Saturday line out the door, and her two younger coworkers frantically trying to keep up.

"Oh Lu, we're so glad you're here! It's been like this since we opened. We're running low on prepped veggies," Amanda said.

Too tired to risk slicing off her finger, Lu responded, "I'll take over at the register and you can do prep." She made her way behind the counter and switched off with her coworker.

After three hours taking orders for kale and carrot smoothies, the morning and lunch rushes were over and one of Lu's coworkers clocked out. The juice bar had been quiet for ten minutes when Lu told Amanda, "It's cool if you take your break. I can handle it on my own for a bit."

Finally alone and still wiped out, Lu leaned on the counter and rested her eyes.

"Um, excuse me," a soft voice said.

Lu opened her eyes to see a woman in her early twenties standing before her. "Oh shit," she mumbled. "Sorry. I was really spent. It got so quiet I must have nodded off. Hope I wasn't drooling."

The woman smiled. "That's okay. I'm sorry I woke you. Late night?"

Lu noticed how inconspicuously beautiful she was: wavy auburn hair, green eyes, and a freckled, porcelain face. "Uh, yeah, late night. I'm a deejay and I was working. I got, like, four hours of sleep."

"Wow, a deejay. That's really cool. Too bad you can't do that full-time."

Lu grimaced. "Uh, yeah. Too bad for me."

The woman blushed. "That came out wrong. I'm so embarrassed! I always say the wrong thing," she said, biting her lip. "I just meant it must be hard having a day job and a night job."

"Yeah, it's hard, but who doesn't have it hard, right?" Lu replied.

She smiled awkwardly. "My name's Paisley."

"I'm Lu. Well, Paisley, you must have come in for a juice or smoothie. What can I make for you?"

"Oh sure, right. I wanted a smoothie – something sweet. What's good?"

"The Tropical, Mango Sunrise, and Strawberry Star are all sweet."

"I'll go with the strawberry one, please."

A few customers came in while Lu made the drink.

"Here you go," Lu said, handing her the pretty pink concoction.

Paisley unzipped her purse, but Lu stopped her. "It's on me, since you had to wake me up and all. Plus, I was a giant grump."

"Oh, that's okay…"

"It's no problem. Enjoy," Lu said.

"Well, thanks. Uh, I hope you get to rest when you get off."

"No can do. I'm working at Club 47 in Hollywood tonight. I'll crash tomorrow."

Paisley started walking out, sidestepping her way to the door, looking at Lu.

"What can I get you?" Lu asked the next customer. She tried to focus on his order, but she couldn't help but glance over to watch Paisley leave.

CHAPTER 3

Tash slowly opened her eyes, squinting to avoid the bright sun. Aidan was already awake, smiling at her, his bleached hair in spikes. "Hey, beauty queen," he whispered.

She looked into his evergreen eyes and gently touched the piercing on his right eyebrow. "How long have you been up?"

"Just a few minutes. It's almost noon."

"Shit," she mumbled.

"Doesn't matter. We have the day to ourselves. Plenty of time," he said, cuddling closer to her.

"Don't forget we're going to that club in West Hollywood tonight. It's Lu's first time headlining there on a Saturday. It's a big deal for her."

"Tonight? Really?"

"Yes, really. I promised. We need to support her," Tash said.

"I work with her all the time. She won't care if we're there, trust me."

"You don't want her to think you're a jerk, abandoning her now that you're almost famous. Plus, it'll be fun."

"I thought we might do something quiet, just the two of us," Aidan said.

"I don't do quiet."

Aidan laughed. "Okay, you got me there. I'll make some coffee and breakfast and then we can figure out the day. Your choice. Maybe the Getty, or the beach. Soon it'll be too hot. Gotta say, I won't miss that."

Tash rolled to her side, sat on the edge of the bed, and slipped her robe on. "I'm just gonna have a yogurt, but coffee would be good."

Aidan leaned toward her, putting his hand on her back. "Hey…"

She leapt up. "The Getty Center," she called back. "I'm jumping in the shower. Bring me coffee when it's ready, okay?"

"Yeah, sure."

Tash went into the bathroom, put her hands on the sink, and dropped her head forward. She looked up, confronting her reflection. *No, Tash. Don't be pathetic. You're fine.*

***

Tash and Aidan sat on the crowded tram heading up to the Getty Center. It was their favorite place in LA. They had taken this ride many times, but today she noticed people staring at them. Aidan had his headphones on, lost in the beats of his future. Tash looked out at a landscape that not long before they feared would be lost to a wild blaze. She looked at Aidan with thoughts of the past and the future, place and space, swirling in her mind. Aidan squeezed her hand, thrusting her into the present.

They disembarked hand in hand. As expected on a cloudless Saturday, the grounds were teeming with locals and tourists.

"We were lucky to get a spot in the garage," Aidan said.

"Uh huh. We always have good parking karma. I'm starving. Let's grab a bite."

"Actually, I made a reservation at the swanky restaurant," Aidan replied, raising his eyebrows.

Tash contorted her face.

"I made it weeks ago, in case we wound up here today. When you were in the shower, I called to push it back. They're holding a window table for us, but we're about fifteen minutes late so we should hustle."

"We usually grab something to-go and sit on the lawn," Tash said.

"Yeah, but I thought this should be special. Besides, we can finally afford nicer things. We can walk around outside after. Cool?"

Tash shrugged. "Sure."

Soon they were sitting in the far corner of the dining room, windows on all sides, overlooking spectacular mountain views.

"Wow, they really gave us the best table in the place," Aidan said.

Tash smiled. "You should probably get used to that."

Aidan opened his mouth, but before he could respond, a waitress came over to take their drink orders.

"Could you do us a favor and take a photo of us?" he asked, handing over his phone. Returning his attention to Tash, he whispered, "I want to remember how beautiful you look today."

"You're such a cheeseball," she quipped.

After taking a few shots, the waitress returned his phone and said, "I don't want to bother you and come off all fangirl, but could we take a picture? I love your music."

Aidan blushed. "Thank you. Of course."

He stood up and the waitress retrieved her phone from her pocket and handed it to Tash. After taking a couple of pictures of them, Tash returned her phone, adding, "I'll have a glass of prosecco."

"A seltzer water for me, please," Aidan said.

As she walked away, Tash smirked at Aidan. "At least I can say I always knew you were hot shit, even back when your big gigs were an H&M store and keggers at NYU."

Aidan looked down and laughed. "It's surreal. Whoever thought that someone like Calvin would happen to hear me and that it would snowball into all of this."

"Imagine what it'll be like when your record drops. Aside from your club groupies, most people have only heard your single and you're already a badass at the star table."

"Luckily, I'll be on tour when it streets, too busy to let it distract me. I still can't believe Calvin asked me to open on his US leg."

"I believe it. Your music is dope. I thought that even before I knew you could also sing and play like every freaking instrument." She paused to take a sip of water before continuing. "And you've got that *thing*, anyway. That thing people want to be around."

Aidan reached across the table for her hand. "As long as you want to be around, I'm good."

"You're such a sap," Tash teased.

The waitress delivered their drinks and took their orders. After she left, Tash said, "It's great we're not totally busted anymore. Living in that dump in the boonies was super depressing. I'm way happier in Venice Beach. Using your advance for a down payment on the condo was genius, but now that money is gone. You're getting paid squat on tour if you can't sell your CDs, and like, who buys those anymore? And you won't be getting your regular club money."

"What are you saying?" Aidan asked.

"We're not flush," Tash replied.

"Babe, it's just lunch. And you know I've never cared about money. I want to make music, live my life. I'm cool with having just enough to get by, always have been. You're the one who relentlessly wants more. The way I see it, we caught a huge break. Let's roll with it."

"*You* caught a huge break," Tash muttered.

"Hey," he said, reaching across the table again. "You're talented and passionate. It's going to happen. It just might not be how you expect. That's the trick: being open to whatever way it comes. And it's not like you haven't done anything these past three years in LA. You rocked all those classes and actually made your short film and it's the bomb. No one can take that away from you."

Before Tash could respond, their food was served.

Aidan focused on his plate, cutting into his chicken. After a long silence, he gently said, "You will make this happen, but you gotta find happiness in the work itself again. The rest doesn't matter as much."

"Easy for you to say," she quipped back, taking a bite of her beet salad.

"Hey, you know I've always felt that way. For me, it's all about making music. I'd be happy spinning at a college party like the old days. Everything else is sparkle, as you would say."

"It's different in film. You need money and connections. There's no frat house version. Without funding, it's impossible to keep going. I can't hit my folks up again. I've done everything I can but all I have to show for it is a pile of rejections."

Aidan's face twitched.

"What's that look about? What could I have done differently?"

"After the internship..."

"Don't even fucking start," she shrieked, dropping her fork. "You'll never know what it was like working for that perv."

"Babe, I know. He put you in a horrible position. I still want to smack the hell out of that guy. It infuriates me. Leaving was the right thing, I just wish you could have found something else in the industry."

"Like what? Like giving freaking studio tours? There was nothing else." Tash picked up her fork and took a bite of salad. "You know I ordered this with the dressing on the side. Our waitress must have been too preoccupied making eyes at you to hear me."

"Do you want me to get her and ask them to make you a new one?"

Tash shook her head. "It's fine."

They sat for a moment and Aidan started eating. Tash took a deep breath and looked directly at him. "I'm sorry. I don't want to ruin the day. It's just…"

"Tell me."

"It's really hard. I mean, I could barely fund *Pop Candy* and it's only seven minutes long. And it was rejected from every short film festival I submitted to. Getting into a festival would have helped with the screenwriting grants for the full-length version, but it doesn't look like that's happening either. And…"

"Yeah?"

"And you're leaving," she moaned.

"It's only for the summer. Just a couple of months. I asked you to come with me or meet me on the road."

"You know I can't. Monroe has that Magic Manor thing and I have to do a ton of shit for her. Summer is her big event season."

"This morning you said that you didn't want Lu to think I was abandoning her. You know I'm not abandoning you either, right?" Aidan asked.

"Yeah, I know. It's fine. I'm good on my own. But I could kill you for planning a huge birthday bash for me and not showing up."

"If we didn't have a show that night, I would fly back for it. In a heartbeat."

Tash smiled. "Chill, it's cool. It's just that being dateless at your own birthday party is kinda sad. Plus, with the whole eighties theme we were supposed to go as Jem and Rio. It was gonna be rad."

"Don't worry. My buddies at the club are all over it. I've planned every detail and it's not going to be even a little sad. I'm pumped, actually," he said, smiling widely and laughing. "It's gonna be sooo you. Truly, truly, truly outrageous. You'll love it."

Tash smirked.

"It's gonna be sick, but the summer is more than one night. Try not to get too wrapped up in Monroe's stuff. Don't forget that you took that job to leave time for your film work."

Tash rolled her eyes. "Being rejected doesn't fill as much time as you'd think."

"Remember, be open to whatever form it comes in. That gallery was interested in showing your film. That could be another path."

"Yeah, but I blew them off. Fucking kills me now. At the time, I was so focused on festivals. Everyone in the classes I took said that's the way you do it, that I'd never get future backing for the longer version unless I went that route. But if you're not the professor's pet student, you don't get the support you need for that either."

"There's more than one gallery in town. For that matter, there's no reason you can't pitch to New York galleries, or Boston, Chicago, or a fishing village in Maine. Just sayin.'"

Tash furrowed her brow.

"Okay, well New York at least. My point is that it's truly a piece of art. I mean, it's stylized, totally pop noir like you intended. The black and white with those eighties pops of color – I think it's brilliant. Films like that can do well on the art scene. You know that better than anyone. That's what you said years ago when you first had the idea, before the people here got in your head. Maybe you should let it be what it is and not worry about what it'll lead to. Carve your own path."

"Maybe. Sometimes I think I should just bag it all. I don't know if I want to put myself out there again."

"It's tough, I know, but I remember how happy you were working on it. Even when it wasn't going perfectly, and even during those brutal editing months, you were alive. Just do me a favor and promise you'll think about it."

"I'll think about it," Tash said, reaching her arm across the table. Aidan rubbed her hand.

"I love you," he said.

"I know."

CHAPTER 4

Aidan and Tash circled the block, looking for a parking space.

"Man, everyone's out tonight. Our luck may have run out," Aidan said.

Tash lowered her visor to check her makeup in the mirror. "Just valet."

"It takes forever to get your car when you valet."

"Not for you. They'll totally get your car first and you know it."

"Yeah, I'm not into cutting in front of everyone."

Tash rolled her eyes, flipped the visor up, and turned to face him. "Don't be lame. Besides, you're on the list like everywhere we go. It's the same thing. Ever notice all the people standing in line?"

He laughed. "Can't argue with that. I'll double back around to the front."

"Ooh! You don't have to," Tash said, pointing to a car pulling out.

"Our lucky streak continues," Aidan said.

Minutes later, they were walking toward the club. Tash was wearing black cigarette pants, a white sequin camisole, and black high heels, her long hair curled into large ringlets at the bottom and her lips stained red. Aidan was wearing tight, black leather pants and a white T-shirt with a peace sign. At six feet tall, he was hard to miss, and together, they were impossible to ignore. Tash grabbed his hand as they strolled past the long line of hopefuls waiting for entry. When the bouncer waved them in, Tash grinned and squeezed Aidan's hand. He looked down, smiling like a schoolboy.

They walked into the intimate, moody club. The venue boasted garnet red walls, a large, black, mirrored bar, a VIP room with black leather couches partly obscured by the bar, and to the right, the dance floor. They spotted a few casual friends they knew from the scene and made small talk. Everyone wanted to shake Aidan's hand or was smiling in his direction. The manager invited them for a drink in the VIP room, but they declined. Lu was on the deejay platform, spinning for the crowd on the dance floor. Aidan raised his hand to get her attention. She smiled and pointed at him and back at herself.

"I think she wants you to make a guest appearance," Tash said.

"This is her night. I'm here to be with you."

"Oh look, she just held up two hands. I think she wants you to join her in ten minutes."

Aidan gestured to Lu, and she nodded in confirmation.

"Told ya so," Tash said.

Aidan blushed. "Well, at least I can get you a drink before she puts me to work."

"Damn straight."

***

Tash leaned on the bar, sipping her fruity drink and watching Aidan join Lu on the platform. Lu took the mic and turned the music down. "Hey, I'm takin' a break because I've got a treat for you. Before he heads out on tour, our friend, the kickass A-A-Aidan, is gonna jump up here and do his thing."

There was thunderous applause as the music swelled and Aidan appeared on the stage. With a fist bump to Lu, he put on her headphones and they swapped places. "Glad to be here, LA! Let's do it," he shouted, to more applause.

Lu pushed through the crowd toward Tash when someone touched her shoulder. She turned to see Paisley.

"Uh, hey there," Lu said.

"Paisley, from earlier today."

"Yeah, I remember," Lu said.

"Your music is great."

"Uh, thanks. I'm surprised to see you here."

"Oh, well you mentioned you were working here tonight, and I'd never been, and I thought, well, I thought…"

"It's cool. So, what do you think of our little spot?" Lu asked.

"I like it. When I got here and saw the line, I didn't think I'd get in."

"Sorry about that. If I knew you were coming, I'd have put you on the list. Come to think of it, how did you get in?"

"I gave the bouncer a hundred bucks."

Lu's eyes widened. "Yup, that'll do it."

"So, that guy's your friend?" Paisley asked, gesturing toward Aidan.

"Yeah, you know his music?" Lu asked.

Paisley shook her head.

"Guess you're not into the club scene. He's kind of a superstar around here."

"I'm not really a late-night person," Paisley said, biting her lip.

"What are you into?" Lu asked.

"Theater. I teach drama at a private high school."

"Very cool."

Paisley smiled.

"Where's the school?"

"Malibu. It's right down the road from me. I actually went to school there so it's kind of like I never left high school, which probably sounds a little pathetic. I guess I never really left home either. I'm crashing in my parent's guesthouse."

"You're from Malibu?" Lu asked, her eyes wide again.

"Yeah, why?"

"No reason. Just never thought people were actually *from* Malibu. But hey, teaching drama is dope."

"Yeah, I'm off for the summer now."

"Sweet deal. Do you have a summer gig?"

"No, I try to keep it chill. I do a lot of hiking, I hang out on the beach quite a bit, and my friends and I see a ton of movies."

"That reminds me, I was actually heading to the bar to meet someone."

"Oh, uh…"

"My best friend. She's into film too. The dude deejaying is her BF. They came here to support me tonight and my only chance to connect is while he's covering for me."

"I totally understand. Of course you should go see your friend."

Lu smiled. "You gonna hang?"

Paisley nodded.

"Cool. See ya," Lu said, brushing her hand as she walked away.

***

"So, my drink is almost empty. Did you get lost on the way?" Tash teased.

"There's this chick, Paisley…"

"Yeah, I totally saw. She's pretty."

Lu blushed.

"Oooh, you like her."

"She's probably psycho. I met her at the juice bar today and she just showed up here."

"How did she know where you'd be?"

"I kind of told her."

Tash rolled her eyes.

"It wasn't like that. I was making small talk."

"You're one of the most private people I know. Intel like that doesn't slip out, not from you. I call bullshit."

Lu scrunched her face. "You're such a bitch," she said before laughing.

"She's hot and she's into you. It's not complicated."

"But she's so girly. She ordered a strawberry smoothie. Who orders strawberry past the age of ten?"

"I eat maraschino cherries out of the jar," Tash said.

"Yeah, I know. It's weird."

Tash made a face.

"I didn't want to have to tell you this, but she's from Malibu. Malibu! She's like a real goody-goody; it's written all over her. I'm not feeling that."

"She looks comfortable in your world tonight," Tash said, nodding toward the other side of the club.

Lu whipped around to see Paisley dancing with abandon in the middle of a group of vinyl-clad strangers. Her cheeks reddened.

"Aww… Lu likes a girl," Tash mocked.

"Forget about me and the goody-goody girl. What about you and your guy? Why the hell are you here tonight? Shouldn't you be spending this time alone together?"

Tash's face fell.

"Babe, it's only like two and a half months. He'll be back before you know it."

"I know. Just didn't want to do the dramatic last-night thing. It's such a downer."

Lu rubbed Tash's arm. "Try to have a good night. This club has one of the sickest vibes in the city."

"I always think this place is so un-LA. It's missing the sanitized, canned happy thing."

"Funny, that's why I think it's the *most* LA of all the clubs I play; it's the underbelly, you know?"

Tash shrugged.

"Well, I'm gonna run for a bathroom break and then relieve your man. Get another drink and try to have fun."

"Yup, I'm the party girl," she said sarcastically.

"I'm off tomorrow if you want to hang after he leaves. Just need some shut-eye first. Text me."

Tash nodded.

"See ya, babe."

"Bye, baby."

***

Tash and Aidan got home at two o'clock in the morning. Tash kicked off her heels and announced, "I'm gonna get ready for bed."

"I'm starving. You want eggs or something?" Aidan asked, grabbing a fistful of Lucky Charms cereal.

"Sure. Sunnyside."

Tash shut the bathroom door and stood still for a moment, breathing deeply. She changed into her robe, put her hair in a ponytail, and washed her face. When she emerged from the bathroom, Aidan called, "Food's up."

Tash plopped down opposite him, crossed her legs on the chair, and sprinkled a little salt on her eggs. She dunked a piece of toast in the yolk, watching it ooze around her plate.

"You're gonna miss my late-night meals," Aidan said, crunching into a piece of buttered toast.

"I'll manage."

"Try to eat something more than cereal and soup from a can," he said with a laugh.

"Hey, I can survive on potato chips and cheese doodles if I have to," Tash joked.

Aidan smiled. "I know you can take care of yourself. I guess I'm just really gonna miss taking care of you, too."

After eating and brushing their teeth, they got into bed and turned off the lights. Aidan lay behind Tash, wrapping his arms around her. "It's really late," she whispered. "You don't want to miss your flight tomorrow."

"Okay, beauty queen. Sweet dreams."

"Good night."

***

Lu unlocked the door to her apartment and let Paisley in. "It's a mess. I wasn't expecting company."

"That's okay. Your place is really cute," she said, looking around. "I like your posters."

"Thanks. Got them all from indie music stores back in the day. Most of them are limited edition promo posters that I begged them to give me when they were done with them. They actually toss most of those."

"That's cool," Paisley said, inspecting an old Cocteau Twins poster.

"Thanks for sticking around the club all night. I hope you weren't bored out of your mind."

"I had a great time. I liked watching you work. You get really intense."

"Speaking of, I'm kind of sweaty and gross. I'm gonna take a quick shower, okay? Help yourself to a beer or water or something."

Paisley smiled.

Lu closed the bathroom door behind her, quickly taking her clothes off and tossing them in the corner. She flipped the shower on. *Please, let it be hot. Ah, yes!* She jumped in and let the water beat on her head, streaming down her body. Her eyes were shut when she felt hands slip around her waist. She opened her eyes to find Paisley in the shower with her. Lu gently touched her face and leaned in to kiss her.

***

Just before dawn, Tash rolled around in bed. When she turned to face Aidan, he put his hand on the back of her head.

"Hey, you," he whispered.

"Hey."

They stared into each other's eyes for a long moment. Tash moved closer to him, gently caressing his forehead. He pulled her head to him and they began passionately kissing. Soon they were making love, with eyes wide open. After, Tash nestled into Aidan. "You smell good," she whispered, before falling asleep cradled in his arms.

A couple of hours later, the alarm woke them both.

"Shit, I gotta get moving," Aidan mumbled.

"Do you want me to make coffee?" Tash asked.

"Nah, I'll grab some at LAX. I'm gonna hop in the shower."

He leapt up and headed to the bathroom. Tash scrunched up the sheet, pulling it to her chest, and closed her eyes.

The next time she awoke, Aidan was sitting on the edge of the bed, softly saying, "My ride's gonna be here in five."

Tash groaned. "I'll throw on sweats."

"Stay in bed."

"No. Hang on," she said.

Aidan got up and retrieved a pair of sweatpants and an old NYU sweatshirt. Tash dragged herself out of bed and slipped them on.

"Okay, let's roll," Aidan said, grabbing his supersized duffel bag and backpack.

Tash scooped up her keys from the mail table and followed him out. Aidan's friend was already waiting for him at the curb. He loaded up the car and turned to Tash.

"You should've let me drive you," she said.

"It would be a waste of your time. Enjoy the day and having the car to yourself this summer. I'll text or FaceTime you when I get there."

"Have a good flight."

"I'll miss you so much."

"Yeah, me too. This is really a big deal for you; have the time of your life. Don't worry about me."

"You're gonna have a great summer, too. Keep working on your film stuff. And stay out of trouble."

Tash rolled her eyes.

"I love you," Aidan said.

Tash smiled, tilting her chin forward; a silent me too.

Aidan got in the car and looked out the window. Tash stood there and watched the car disappear down the street.

As she walked back toward the apartment complex, she saw Darrell leaving his apartment, pulling a wagon loaded with paintings. She waved and he nodded in acknowledgment.

Shoulders slumped, she entered her quiet apartment, dropped her keys on the table, and shuffled into the bedroom. She took off her sweatpants and crawled into bed, pulling the covers up. She inhaled deeply. *It still smells like him.*

CHAPTER 5

Lu's eyelids flitted open and closed, like a butterfly scrambling to take flight. She saw flickers of Paisley, bathed in sunlight, each time her eyes opened.

"You passed out. You must have been really wiped," Paisley said.

"Yeah, I slept hard," Lu muttered. "What time is it?"

"It's almost two."

"Damn," Lu mumbled, stretching her arms and pulling herself up to a sitting position. "I'm sorry if you felt kept hostage. You could have bailed."

"That's okay. I snagged one of your books about the East Village in the 1970s and '80s."

"Cool stuff, eh?"

"Totally. I'll have to maybe borrow it to finish, if that's okay."

"Sure," Lu grumbled through a yawn. "You must be starving," she said, her own stomach growling.

"I had a granola bar. I hope you don't mind. I wanted to make you something to eat, but…"

"Yeah, haven't been to the store in a while."

"If you're busy and you want me to go…"

"No, not at all," Lu said, reaching for a shirt on the floor. "Maybe we can grab a bite. There's an all-day breakfast place nearby."

"Breakfast every hour, it could save the world," Paisley said.

Lu furrowed her brow.

"It's the lyric of a song."

"Ah, yeah. Old Tori Amos, right?"

"Uh huh."

"Cool. I like the musical free association."

Paisley smiled.

"So, you up for some chow?"

Paisley nodded.

"I'm gonna run to the bathroom. Hang tight."

When Lu re-emerged, her hair was damp and she was humming.

"Well you're bright and shiny," Paisley said, seated on the edge of the bed with the book open on her lap.

"Yeah. My mind's been all blocked up for days and it finally feels clear."

Paisley stood up as Lu walked over, the book falling to the floor. Lu took her hand and said, "And last night…"

"Yeah, last night," Paisley said softly, biting her lip. They stared at each other before Paisley took a deep breath and continued, "Well, I guess you must be hungry."

Lu touched the side of her face. "Food can wait."

***

Paisley was still scouring the laminated menu when the waitress came over.

Lu leaned in. "Do you know what you want?"

"You go first," Paisley said.

"I'll have the sausage breakfast sandwich and a coffee," Lu said. "The sausage here is homemade. It's awesome," she said to Paisley.

"Uh, can I please have an egg white omelet with spinach, no dairy, with fruit and coffee?"

"Toast and home fries? Comes with," the waitress queried.

"No, thank you."

"I'll have hers," Lu said, handing her both menus. She then turned her attention to Paisley. "I'm starving."

Paisley giggled and coyly tilted her head. "Well, I guess I'm kinda to blame for that."

Lu smiled. "You're blushing."

Paisley looked down, her cheeks getting redder by the minute.

"This place is kind of great, huh? Totally kitsch."

"Uh huh," Paisley responded, still blushing.

Lu reached her hand across the table, but before she made contact the waitress delivered two cups of coffee. "Ah, thank you!" Lu said, immediately dumping cream into her cup. She held out the creamer.

"Oh, no thanks. I drink it black."

Lu gulped her coffee. "Lactose intolerant? I noticed you asked for no dairy in your omelet."

"I used to be vegan. I still try to keep as close to vegan as I can, but I do eat eggs sometimes. I know it's such an LA cliché. It's my mom; she's a total 'paint with all the colors of the wind' hippie and raised me that way."

"Is it totally gross to you that I ordered sausage?"

"Not at all. I'm not like that."

Lu sipped her coffee again. "So, your mom is a hippie living in a Malibu estate. How'd that happen?"

"She was in the music business, a producer, big in the nineties. She got in early on a lot of things and developed really nurturing relationships with a bunch of musicians. They were loyal to her. Grunge, hip-hop, the folk singer renaissance, she had a hand in everything. She spends most of her time now doing yoga and gardening."

"Wow," Lu said, her eyebrows raised. "That's dope."

"My mom's great, really supportive. We're close. I know it's sorta lame, but she's my best friend. She's from Newport Beach and grew up in this very white-bread, corporate kind of family. Not super rich, but upper-middle class. She was like this Bohemian chick that didn't quite fit in. My dad is a hippie at heart, but he's a computer geek and hit it big in tech. They're two of the mellowest people you could ever meet, but they've had these massive careers in intense industries. That's how they ended up in Malibu."

The waitress delivered their food, with the toast and home fries on a separate plate for Lu. Lu picked up her sandwich and took a bite. She moaned as she chewed. "Sorry, this is so good."

Paisley smiled, taking a bite of her cantaloupe. "What about you?"

"What about me?" Lu asked, taking another bite.

"You're not from LA. I'm guessing you came here for the music scene."

Lu nodded as she took a forkful of home fries.

"Where are you from? Where else have you lived?"

Lu chugged her water. "I'm from the Midwest, which felt like the middle of nowhere. Lived in Seattle before I came here. It was pretty cool."

"How'd you end up in Seattle?"

"My girlfriend at the time, Jenna. She was a couple of years older than me and was moving to the Pacific Northwest. Totally granola. She wanted to go to Portland to live on a commune or some shit, but I convinced her to go to Seattle instead. I figured it would be easier to get into music there."

"Was it?" Paisley asked, taking a bite of her omelet.

Lu shook her head. "I worked in a coffee shop. I was just buying time before I could make it here."

"What about Jenna? She didn't want to come?"

"We broke up. I left her, actually."

"Oh," Paisley said, taking a sip of coffee.

"I was never serious about her like she was about me. Don't get me wrong – she was a beautiful person." Lu paused and then added, "Honestly, she was a getaway car."

"What were you trying to get away from?"

"Everything," Lu said, picking up her sandwich and taking a hearty bite.

***

Tash looked at her newly organized closet and shook her head. *I should have some outfits ready to go for days that I'm running late.* For the third time that afternoon, she removed every hanger from her closet, piling clothes on her bed. This time, she paired some pants and tops together on a single hanger. She then rifled through her jewelry drawer, taking out necklaces and bracelets to hold up against each outfit. After a long process of trying each piece of jewelry with each outfit, she wrapped the selected jewelry around the hook of each hanger. She then rehung everything in her closet, beginning with outfits on one end and single items on the other. After reviewing her work, she made a few final adjustments, grouping similar colors and similarly weighted clothes. She felt proud of herself but then inadvertently glanced at

Aidan's side of the closet and sighed. *I should start on my dresser*, she thought.

Half an hour into organizing her underwear drawer, her phone beeped with a message from Lu.

```
Hey. Slept half the day. Wanted to
check in. What are you up to?
Color coding my bras
Fuck. I'm coming over. You have food
there?
A little
Booze?
Yeah
See you in an hour
```

***

Lu showed up at Tash's with a grocery bag in one hand and a glittery cardboard tiara in the other. She held out the tiara.

Tash smiled as she put it on.

"I figured you could use a little sparkle," Lu said, walking past her toward the kitchen.

"I'm really fine," Tash said.

"Great, then you can help me make dinner."

Tash followed Lu into the kitchen and watched her unload spaghetti, crushed tomatoes, garlic, broccoli, maraschino cherries, and mini marshmallows.

Tash grabbed the jar of cherries and simpered. "But what's up with the marshmallows?"

"They're my thing. I usually indulge in private. I'll be weird with you."

Tash smiled.

"Oh, totally random, but I saw your neighbor, that painter dude, on the pier a few days ago."

"Darrell. Yeah, he sells his art there sometimes, 'til the cops chase him away. I saw him this morning with a wagon full of paintings, probably heading there."

"His stuff is pretty haunting. The eyes in the faces, like *wow*. What's his story?"

"I don't really know. He's kind of a loner."

"Hey, I need a large pot with a lid and a sauté pan," Lu said, poking through cabinets.

"Down there," Tash said, pointing.

"Great," Lu said and retrieved the items. "Do you have a colander to drain the pasta? And where do you keep olive oil and spices?"

"Oil and spices are over there," Tash said, pointing again.

Lu perused the selection of spices and dried herbs. "Nice spread, all organic."

"Aidan's kinda into cooking," she replied, as she grabbed the colander from an upper cabinet.

"You heard from him?" Lu asked, as she filled the pot with water.

"Got a text when he landed. He sent me a cheesy picture we took at the Getty yesterday."

"Cool. Open a bottle of wine and then you can help me peel garlic."

***

Tash swirled the spaghetti around her fork, using a spoon. "This smells so good," she said, before taking a big bite.

"It's one of the few recipes I've mastered," Lu said, sipping her Merlot.

"It's got a kick. You're such a badass, even in the kitchen. It's really good," Tash said, dragging a piece of broccoli through the extra sauce on her plate.

"Chili flakes. You know me, I like a surprise," Lu said.

"Oh hey, speaking of surprises, what happened with that chick last night, the goody-goody girl?"

Lu's face turned red.

"Oooh, you can't even speak," Tash teased.

"I'm chewing," Lu said, covering her full mouth with her hand.

Tash shook her head. "Come on, give me the dirt."

"She came home with me and…" Lu trailed off.

"And?" Tash prodded.

"I jumped in the shower because I was gross from work…"

"Oh my god, she surprised you naked in the shower?" Tash asked, her eyes like saucers. "I told you she looked at home in your world. Not such a goody-goody, huh?"

Lu laughed. "Uh, yeah, she did," she said, looking down and smiling. "It was amazing. We just clicked, you know? We had this intense chemistry. And then today, again…"

"You are beet red!"

"I didn't expect to like her so much. She's such a sweetheart, really soft, you know? She's into art and she loves the outdoors. It's been a while since I've felt this, if ever, really. Caught me off guard."

Tash smiled.

"We went to Mandy's for a late breakfast and…"

"Yeah?"

"I don't know. She wanted to do the whole 'tell me your life' thing. No surprise, her life has been all shades of rosy. Like seriously freaking perfect. It's just not me. Plus, I mentioned Jenna and probably scared her."

"You never tell anyone about Jenna."

"It was nothing. She asked me where I lived before, that's all. I have her number, but I'm not sure. I don't have time for a big thing. She's definitely not the casual type."

Tash dropped her fork, rested her chin in her hand, and stared at Lu.

"What?" Lu asked, taking a sip of wine.

"Look, I get it. I do, more than you know. But she's hot and you have a connection. Let go of your shit and see what happens."

Lu shrugged. "Speaking of letting go of shit, what's with the spring cleaning?"

"Slept late after he left. Felt like staying home. At least I got something done."

"Fair enough. You working tomorrow?" Lu asked, before taking a bite of pasta.

"Monroe is having 'something done,' so she doesn't need me until Tuesday."

"Not what I mean. You working tomorrow?"

Tash poured more wine in both of their glasses.

Lu tilted her head, sympathetically. "Look, I get it. Maybe more than *you* know. Do you want to talk about what's really going on here?"

"No. Do you?" Tash asked.

Lu took a sip of wine.

Tash stood up. "I'm gonna get more sauce, it's really good."

CHAPTER 6

Tash usually sped through Monroe's neighborhood, but today as she drove down the palm tree lined streets of Beverly Hills, she slowed down to take stock of each home. *That one's a garish monstrosity. What are they trying to prove? You're rich, new money, we get it. Ew, the next one's even worse. Why do the super rich have such bad taste? Oh, that one's pretty sick. Great throwback vibe. I can imagine the kind of person that lives there. Probably someone from the industry, a director from back in the day or a once-upon-a-time red carpet darling. Being a washed up star must be a mindfuck. And they all fall or fade. To get something you've chased, to live the dream, knowing it won't last and then having that truth come to pass. Maybe it's not an industry suited to happiness, just the pursuit.* Her thoughts turned to her own pursuit of happiness. *Can't believe I lost all of yesterday vegging in bed. I should be making movies, not watching them. Aidan would give me so much shit. What's my problem? I'm sliding back into who I used to be. Didn't think I'd ever go back. Fuck. Snap out of it, T. Get back to it. Okay, a couple of hours with Monroe and then when I get home, I'll work. I just need to get into it again.*

Tash's thoughts settled as she pulled into Monroe's driveway. She hopped out into the blazing LA sunshine to see Henry standing outside, speaking with the gardener.

"Yo, H," Tash called.

"Good afternoon, Miss Daniels. You'll find Mrs. Preston by the pool."

Tash waved as she walked around to the back of the estate. She spotted Monroe in the distance on the upper terrace, dressed in a white sundress, large white hat, and black sunglasses. She was seated under an umbrella at one end of the long teak table, reading as usual.

Tash walked on the pathway along the pool's edge, past the red, yellow, and purple flower beds, and then up the stairs to the sprawling terrace that ran along the backside of the estate. As she approached, Monroe looked up from her book and smiled. Tash immediately noticed her lips were poutier than usual. *Ah, so that's what she did.*

"What are you reading, another Oprah pick?" Tash asked, as she took a seat.

"It's supposed to be one of those soul-enriching books. It's on the bestseller list, but so far it's nothing more than clichés and empty platitudes, as far as I can tell at least."

Tash smiled, thinking that Monroe was much wiser than most people probably assumed.

"How was your weekend? Did the clothes work out for your events?" Tash asked.

"I received compliments all weekend, especially on that jumpsuit. I never would have chosen that without you, but you were right, it was so comfortable. You have such a good eye. I've always loved to dress up, but I never had a real knack for fashion."

"You're getting there," Tash said. "You could do this on your own."

"People keep asking who my stylist is. Is it terrible I don't want to share my secret?"

Tash laughed. "I'm all yours."

A member of the kitchen staff brought over a tray carrying their lunch: two pristine butter lettuce salads topped with avocado and crab salad and garnished with fish roe, a mineral water for Monroe, and a diet cola for Tash.

"Thank you," Monroe said. "I remembered how much you enjoyed the crab puffs the cook made. I thought this would be refreshing on a hot day."

"Looks great," Tash replied, taking a bite of the tarragon-laced crab.

"How was your weekend?" Monroe asked, sipping her water.

"Uh, it was all right. Aidan left to go on that tour, so…"

"That's right! It's exciting what's happening for him. He's really made it. I was talking with one of my girlfriends and she knew his music, her son is a fan. I may have to ask you for an autographed picture or something someday."

"Sure."

"I have to confess: I looked online and wow, he's gorgeous. What a jawline. He looks like he was born for this. He has that indescribable *thing*. Your lives must be changing so quickly."

Tash sighed.

"Oh dear, I'm sorry. You must miss him."

"Yeah, I miss him, but I'm cool with him doing what he needs to do." She paused before continuing, "It's really his life that's changing, not mine."

Monroe took a breath, looking at her sympathetically. "I've had to come to terms with some things about Bill's world over the years. When a studio head is in the room, no one else is. It's about power. They all want something from him."

Tash put her fork down. "Can I ask you a personal question?"

"Yes."

"You look like a star, truly, you're crazy beautiful. I always wondered if you came to LA to be an actress or something."

Monroe smiled ever so slightly. "I wanted a grand life, more than anything. Of course, it was just a fantasy, but I was headstrong about making it happen. When I was a teenager, I watched a lot of eighties nighttime soap operas. The fashion and opulence blew my mind. My mother and I argued about them; she didn't care for those shows and we only had one television."

Tash smiled. "That's so funny. I'm obsessed with eighties pop culture. Love it. It influences my work."

"Then you understand the allure. I also watched old movies and fell in love with the stars of the 1940s and '50s. I mean that in the truest sense. Deeply in love with them. I guess I developed an idea of old Hollywood meets contemporary glamour, or at least what was contemporary at the time. I knew I'd get myself here, come hell or high water, to the land of palm trees and silver screen dreams." With a giggle, she added, "Mind you, I had no real talent or even passion for acting, but I thought it would fall into place if I could only get here."

"Did it?" Tash asked.

"I was living with a bunch of girls, models who were all waitressing or doing odd jobs on the side. I modeled for a bit. I didn't have much luck because of my body type. Thin was in and I was too voluptuous. All I could book were lingerie shoots. It wasn't glamorous in the least. The adult industry was interested, but that wasn't for me. Eventually, I gave up and took a job as a hostess at a chichi industry restaurant. One night, a VIP came in with a large group. You could tell he was important because everyone fawned over him. It sounds naïve, but I was drawn to him because of his sweet eyes. The most powerful man in the room had the gentlest eyes. He was taken with me too. He asked for my number that night, but I said no."

"Why?"

"I was so young, only twenty at the time. He was twice my age. I thought he was out of my league and I didn't want to be his girl of the week. My mother had warned me about that sort of thing and that sort of man. But he pursued me for weeks and eventually I said yes. It was a whirlwind romance and we got married ten months later. No one thought it would last, which I can understand, but here we are a quarter of a century later. We had a connection. It was easy. He always says I bring him joy, which is strange to me," she said, her eyes distant.

Tash cocked her head. "In a way, that kind of reminds me of my relationship with Aidan. We both like the lighter side of life. We gel."

Monroe smiled, pensively.

Tash continued, "What about acting? Since he's in the film industry, did you ever ask him to get you a part or an audition or something?"

"Never. Because of him, I met everyone. When I was young, many offered me small parts or representation. I always said I wasn't interested. I was tempted once, in the very beginning. We were at a party and I met the man who owned Guess. He asked me to do a test shoot. He said I looked like a modern-day Marilyn Monroe and he wanted me to be their next model. Guess girls became very famous at that time. I admit getting a little swept up by the idea."

"You didn't pursue it?"

Monroe gazed down and then looked confidently at Tash. "Our lives were busy with professional commitments, and Bill thought I would enjoy charity work, which turned out to be mostly hosting parties. I took some classes, too. Sculpture, watercolors, I even took theology and philosophy in a continuing education program." She stared into the distance for a moment before continuing. "And I was adjusting to all of it, which took time. This life, even though I wanted it, I suppose it isn't natural for me. I had never known a world like this.

Just getting rid of my southern accent took ages, and it still creeps in a bit." She paused again for a moment before concluding, "Besides, I never had any real talent, just a dream for something glamorous."

Tash looked around at the house and grounds. "Seems like your dream came true."

"Hmm, I suppose it did. Funny how things are often different than we imagine. We never know what form our dreams will take."

"Yeah, I've actually been thinking about that a lot lately."

Monroe smiled and sipped her water. "What about your short film? I didn't realize it was influenced by the eighties."

"Yeah, it's black and white with eighties-inspired pops of color."

"You haven't mentioned it in ages. Did you screen it at festivals?"

Tash shook her head. "That didn't work out. I've been hoping to write a feature-length version, but…"

"I'd love to see it sometime, your short film," Monroe said.

"Sure. I'll bring it by. Well, should we start on the garden party gifts? I have some ideas I think you'll like."

***

Lu picked up the cutting board to wipe off the carrot peels. She dropped the carrots into the bin and then started on the beets. Amanda turned around from the register and hollered, "Strawberry Star and Tropical Blend up next."

Lu's heart raced. She turned to the counter, but it was just a couple of kids. She made the drinks and then tried to wash the stains off her hands before saying, "Hey, Amanda, we're low on kale. If you can handle it up here for a minute, I'll go back and clean some."

"Okay."

Lu made her way to the backroom, gathered a pile of kale from the refrigerator, and threw it on the counter. She grabbed her backpack and took out her phone. She shut her eyes, shook her head, and then texted Paisley:

> Hey. Sorry I didn't call yesterday.
> Busy. I'm off tomorrow. Wanna go for
> a hike or hit the beach?

She slid her phone into her pocket and started cleaning the kale. Ten minutes later, her phone beeped.

> Let's go for a hike. Should I pick you
> up at 10? I'll pack snacks.

Lu smiled. *Damn, she's too sweet.*

***

Tash got home at the end of the afternoon, threw her keys on the entry table, and walked into the kitchen. She opened the refrigerator and mindlessly scanned the contents. Not really hungry, she opened the maraschino cherry jar and popped one in her mouth. The sweet, squishy burst soothed her.

She went into her room and changed into sweats and a tank top. Her laptop was on her dresser, taunting her. *Get your shit together.* She climbed into bed with her computer. Waiting for it to boot up, she thought about Monroe. *She has everything people dream of, but there was something in her eyes, like she wonders what else she could have had, wonders where she'd be had she gone for that modeling job. Hard to imagine her life could be any better than it is. I guess we all have many lives: the one we live and the ones we might have lived.*

Staring at her desktop, she looked at her grant application folder, her writing folder, and the link to her film. She hovered the mouse over each one as a lump formed in her throat. *Fuck it*, she thought, slamming the laptop shut. She fetched the remote control from the nightstand, flicked on the television, and nestled under the comforter. *His smell is fading.*

PART TWO

CHAPTER 7

Monroe Preston had slept peacefully virtually every night since her wedding day. It didn't matter whether her husband was traveling or lying beside her in one of their many homes, free from the anxieties and to-do lists that kept most people spinning in their own heads, she shut her eyes each night and quickly drifted off to sleep. Until tonight.

Monroe lay awake nearly all night, her silk nightgown soft against her one-thousand-count sateen sheets. Something indiscernible wasn't quite right, or perhaps, she feared, she wasn't quite right. Listening to Bill breathing, she stared at the ceiling thirty feet above. She remembered being a young girl, lying awake in bed and counting the glow-in-the-dark stars she stuck on her ceiling, dreaming of her big life and no longer being Jenny Anne Foster from the south of nowhere. Suddenly, the county talent show flashed before her eyes.

"Mama, do I look all right?" she asked, twirling in front of the mirror, examining her silver sequined dress.

"You look like tinsel sparkling under twinkly lights. Lucky thing I'm good with a needle and thread, isn't it, since you love to dress up? Come on now, grab your baton. They're gonna call you next."

Moments after her performance she ran backstage, where her mother was waiting with open arms. "Now I warned you to practice more." She sighed before continuing, "Don't feel too bad, Jenny Anne. Everyone drops the baton sometimes."

"I don't feel bad, Mama. Did you hear the applause? They loved the dress you made me. It sparkled even brighter under the stage lights."

"Well of course they loved it. Who doesn't like tinsel in twinkly lights, sweet girl?"

With a slight snore, Bill rolled over, interrupting her thoughts and flinging her into the present. When he was settled, she let her mind wander back to how it felt standing center stage, and then to her mother's words. "You look like tinsel sparkling under twinkly lights."

That's all I wanted, Mama, to sparkle in Tinseltown. And here I am. But nothing is quite as I imagined.

***

Even when Bill was in town, Monroe rarely saw him in the morning. His car always picked him up hours before she'd rise. So, when he tried to slip out of bed, quietly as usual, he was surprised when she whispered, "Good morning."

"Did I wake you?"

"I've been up for ages." He started to walk toward their master bathroom when she said, "Did I tell you Tash's boyfriend got a record deal?"

"Wow. That's great."

"He's on tour," Monroe added, sitting up.

"Uh huh," Bill replied, walking into the bathroom.

"He might really make it. Isn't that something?"

"Uh huh," Bill mumbled.

"Bill, I was thinking about the funniest thing," she hollered.

"Come in here," he replied.

She slipped on her silk robe and sashayed to the bathroom doorway. Bill stood at the marble vanity, brushing his teeth.

"I was thinking about that offer I got to model for Guess. Do you remember that?"

He switched his electric toothbrush off and turned to face her.

"I remember. Seems like another lifetime. What made you think of that?"

"Oh, I don't know. Tash asked me if I'd wanted to be an actress. We were chatting about why I came to California."

"With regret or nostalgia?"

She blinked and shook her head. "Do you ever wonder what it would have been like if I modeled or acted?"

"You hated modeling. When we were dating, you told me such horror stories."

Monroe shrugged. "I suppose that's true. Well, acting then. A lot of people offered me things when we were first married. Remember? You discouraged it."

Bill crinkled his face. "I remember the offers. You never seemed interested. You told me you'd never even been in a high school play."

"Yeah, I guess."

He put his toothbrush down and folded his arms. "What's going on? Do you wish you had…"

"I'm being silly. I didn't act, you're right. I was just wondering 'what if,' I guess."

Bill walked over and kissed the top of her head.

"I'll let you get ready for your day," she said, closing the bathroom door.

***

An hour later, alone again, Monroe looked in the bathroom mirror, inspecting her freshly washed skin. After spraying her face with hydrating mist and gently rubbing in SPF moisturizer, she examined her newly plumped lips, pouting and releasing several times before concluding they still appeared natural. She couldn't shake her conversation with Tash. *It's been years since I've thought about those early days in California. I do wonder how things would be different if I had gone to that test shoot, or taken one of those other roles. Bill is right, though. I didn't have any real interest after I met him, just a curiosity or fantasy. And now that I've seen the other side, what their lives are really like, celebrity has lost its luster. I hope Tash is all right. She must be afraid her boyfriend will leave her. Maybe she's afraid of having to choose between his dream and hers. Or that his dream will eclipse hers, slowly becoming her own, before she can notice. Our choices always have shadow sides. Like I told her, dreams never come to us quite the way we expect.* Fluffing her platinum hair with her fingers, she remembered the first time she and her best friend Lauren tried to dye it, at the age of fifteen.

"My mother's gonna kill me if I ruin the towels."

"I'll help you clean up. Jenny Anne, you're gonna look like a movie star. You're already the prettiest girl in school," Lauren said.

"Do you really think I could be a movie star?"

"Definitely!"

"Oh, I don't know, there are lots of pretty girls. But it sure would be exciting to be famous and have everything you ever could want. To have people admire you. Don't tell anyone, but I've been thinking about changing my name to something that stands out, just like Marilyn Monroe did."

"I bet you'll look just like her when your hair is done."

"Maybe I should call myself Monroe. You know, as my first name."

"That's so cool. You should do it. Change your name as soon as you're eighteen and then go to Hollywood. Maybe I can be your assistant or makeup artist or something, if we're still friends," Lauren said, adjusting her wire-rimmed glasses.

"Of course we'll still be friends!"

"Oooh, the timer! Let's wash your hair."

Twenty minutes later, as she finished blow drying her hair, disappointment set in. Lauren tried to console her. "It's not exactly what you wanted but it's not that bad. It's kind of auburn-ish."

"It's not blonde like the woman on the box at all. I don't know what we did wrong. It's still dark brown, but now it has a reddish glow. It's awful," she whined.

Lauren comforted her as best as she could, reminding her she was still the most beautiful girl she had ever seen in real life.

Months later, after saving every penny she earned from her new after-school job at a local grocery store, she went to the fanciest salon in three counties where she learned it wasn't simple to go from dark to light hair. Her wish would take time and money. After a few visits, she gazed into the salon mirror to finally see the hair of her dreams reflected back at her.

"Oh wow!" she exclaimed, catching her breath. "I look like *someone*, you know," she said, earnestly.

"Everybody is someone," the stylist replied flatly.

"Uh huh," she muttered, admiring her transformation.

She bounded home to show off her new coif. Her mother wasn't impressed.

"Jenny Anne, most girls would kill to look like you just the way you are. You don't need to keep doing these things to attract attention."

"Mama, I want to stand out, to be in the spotlight. Don't you ever imagine a glamorous life? That's what I'm going to have. My life will be grand, you'll see."

Her mother leaned closer and gently touched her hair, grimacing. "You're young. You'll have different priorities someday."

"Like sewing until my fingers bleed, just to scrape by? Like sitting alone night after night in a house with more paint chipped off than is left on?"

Her mother, who always had a quietness, looked at her sharply.

"I'm sorry, Mama. I didn't mean it like that. But was your dream really to sew hems and make dresses for other women? Don't you want a closet of dresses of your own, and fabulous parties to wear them to?"

Her mother softly said, "Fancy dresses and parties don't make people happy. Taking care of yourself by doing something simple and useful is nothing to feel ashamed about. You'll see that someday."

"Then why are you so lonely?"

"One thing's got nothing to do with the other," she muttered.

"You don't think I'll make it, that I'll get out of here and do something special."

Her mother shook her head. "You don't hear a word I say. Going, going, going to some big and glitzy life, that's all you ever think about. You don't even act or sing. All you've ever done is baton twirling, and that was only because you liked the costumes I made for you. You didn't even practice. Glamour alone isn't a goal. It isn't a life. You're already plenty special, but I wish you'd get your head out of the clouds, Jenny Anne. Life will disappoint you."

Defiantly, she replied, "Lauren's mom invited me for dinner. They want to see my new hair. I have to go or I'll be late."

"Wipe off some of that makeup first. I don't want her parents thinking I'm permissive. Besides, you're plenty pretty without it."

Monroe continued fluffing her hair, wondering whatever happened to Lauren. *She was so sweet. I feel bad that I never called after I moved.* She glanced at her vanity, covered with top-of-the-line cosmetics, and thought of her mother. She looked over at the small, framed photo she kept next to her wedding photo. "Funny thing is,

Mama, you were right. I bet you'd love that. When you go to bed at night, you wash it all off and have only yourself. I still wish you would have lived long enough to see my life. The thing is, my head was in the clouds because I wanted to be up there with the stars. Nothing wrong with dreaming, Mama. Only bad part of dreaming is waking up. The details start to slip away, and you can try to catch them, to remember, but eventually they fade to black."

***

As she did each morning, Monroe grabbed the book off her nightstand to take to breakfast. She was midway through Sarah Cohen's latest tome and was eager to keep reading. Although she had a full day planned, she uncharacteristically meandered around her house, admiring the exquisite art that lined the walls. She stopped in front of the Andy Warhol rendition of Marilyn Monroe. Bill had bought it at auction for her thirtieth birthday. It was the best present she had ever received. *He said everyone would be famous in the future. Wonder if he ever said anything about being near the famous. It's not quite the same thing, is it Mr. Warhol? And what about you, Marilyn? Poor, haunted Marilyn. It's not so easy to be two people, is it? It's like being no one at all. What did Hollywood do to you? Did fame help you escape Norma Jeane? I guess it wasn't as glamorous as you hoped. I do wonder, though, were you truly and deeply unhappy or did you just wake up one day feeling somehow outside of the moment and outside of yourself?* She ran her fingers along the frame and suddenly had a thought that was entirely new to her. *Could it be that I'm living the shadow side of my own life?*

With this question lingering in her mind, she strolled downstairs and into the sun-kissed breakfast room. The cook promptly served her usual breakfast: Italian roast coffee, fruit, and a soft-boiled egg.

"May I get you anything else, Mrs. Preston?"

"There are some fashion magazines by the pool. I'd like to flip through them before Tash arrives, if you don't mind. Thank you."

The cook set off to retrieve the magazines and Monroe picked up a sterling silver teaspoon and started tapping the top of her egg. As it cracked, her mind veered to her early days in LA and one particularly terrible modeling job. She and another model were in a small backroom the size of a closet. It reeked of bleach and she wondered if it had been the scene of a crime. Monroe leaned against the wall, changing into lingerie two sizes too small when the photographer started screaming for her. The other model warned, "He's impatient." She touched Monroe's shoulder, "He's feely. Watch yourself." Monroe's anxiety grew as she hurried to the set.

"Get on the bed," he snapped.

Anxious but afraid to be perceived as difficult, she sat on the edge of bed.

"Lie on your side."

In a flash, he had her flat on her back. She stared at the cracks in the popcorn ceiling as he hovered over her, his body odor permeating the air.

"On your knees," he barked.

She lifted herself up and he put his camera down beside her.

"Your bosom doesn't look right," he said, placing his hands on the underwire of her bra and manually adjusting her breasts.

Humiliated and wondering why none of the others in the room – assistant, makeup artist, hair stylist – intervened on her behalf, she withstood the manhandling. The other model glanced at her, but quickly averted her eyes. At the end of the shoot, embarrassed and afraid to end up alone with him, she quickly changed and ran out of the building, tripping on the cement stairs and bloodying both knees. When she got home and told her roommates what happened, they just shrugged and insisted "that stuff happens all the time" and she was "lucky it didn't go further." One of the girls, who she suspected was jealous of her, suggested it wasn't surprising because she "looks like a Playboy model" and "only does lingerie jobs, which everyone knows is code for something else." After that experience and repeated pressure to pose nude, she quit modeling. Determined to make LA work if only to prove her mother wrong, she took a job as a cocktail waitress, until months later her friend helped her score a hostess position at a high-end restaurant. Within eight months, she met Bill. As she sat in the breakfast room of their estate, she remembered the moment they met, when he'd stumbled on his own name, unable to take his eyes off her.

She smiled, still able to feel the warmth emanating from him. *He's such a kind and generous man. I've been bathed in his light nearly my whole adult life. I'm luckier than I ever imagined, aren't I?* Lost in thought, she was visibly startled when the cook returned with the magazines.

"I'm sorry, Mrs. Preston. I didn't mean to sneak up on you."

"Oh, that's okay. I don't know where my mind was."

The cook placed the magazines in front of her. "May I get you anything else?"

"I have everything I could want."

CHAPTER 8

"Fuck," Tash grumbled, realizing she was out of coffee filters. *I need caffeine.* As she created a makeshift filter using a paper towel, she remembered her days in New York with Jason and Penelope. *Pen always got so annoyed when I forgot to pick stuff up. Never thought I'd miss her so much. And Jason, oh my God, Snapchat isn't enough. I gotta go to New York and visit him.* As the smell of coffee began to waft through the air, her thoughts turned to her New York college days. *God, I was with some sketchy dudes back then. I was so messed up. Funny thing, as gorgeous as he is, I probably wouldn't have given a guy like Aidan a real chance back then; he's too nice. I would have driven him away, not believing he was for real. Hell, I still almost did that. Can't get over that I thought that loser Jacob was cool. What the fuck, Tash? Asshole thought he'd share me with his lowlife friends, whether I consented or not. Scumbags.* She shuddered, wanting to clear her mind, and snatched her phone for a distraction. There was a text from Aidan.

> Hey, beauty queen. I know you're sleeping, damn time zones. Wanted to say I miss you. FaceTime me tomorrow before 2 my time if you can.

Yeah, I miss you too, she thought, before replying with smiley face emojis. The coffee maker beeped and she filled her mug. *Fuck, there are grounds in it. I used to be good at this.*

***

Tash arrived at Monroe's with a sample invitation from the calligrapher. Monroe held the invitation up to the light and said, "I love how they've made the lettering on the top look like it's disappearing."

"Yeah, it came out great," Tash replied.

"Did I tell you it was my idea?" Monroe asked.

Tash shook her head.

"So, I was hosting a small dinner party for a few of Bill's employees. They were all making suggestions for the studio's anniversary party, typical stuffy parties and tired red-carpet themes. Sometimes people in the industry side of the business forget what it's all about, what draws people here, why we're still mesmerized when we sit in dark theaters, watching larger-than-life people on the screen and imagining our own lives."

Tash smiled, knowingly. "What do you think it is?"

"Magic. And that's what I told them. It wasn't meant as a suggestion, I was just thinking out loud. I said it should be a celebration of movie magic. And what better place to do that than Magic Manor, to put a fun, childlike spin on it?"

"I love it," Tash said.

"It's going to be the social event of August, the whole year really, but very exclusive. We're inviting studio executives and a select few of the actors, writers, and directors from our biggest, award-winning films. I emailed the calligrapher the final guest list this morning."

"Sounds fantastic."

"The studio is handling most of it, but there are still details for us to work out, including the gift bags and, of course, my outfit. I want to get everything settled for the rest of the summer as well. I hate to impose, but can you work some extra hours over the next few weeks? Bill and I decided to spend a couple of weeks at the Santa Barbara ranch house, and I want to make sure everything is taken care of before we leave. You'll have two paid weeks off while I'm away. Possibly more if I can convince him to stay longer."

"No problem. I could use something to keep me busy anyway."

Monroe smiled compassionately. "Okay, let's get started. I clipped some magazine photos. What do you think about a black, strapless gown?"

They worked for a couple of hours before Monroe had to leave for her weekly appointment with an astrologer.

"It's a scorcher today. With your boyfriend away, if you're not in a rush, you should take a dip in the pool and relax before you go," Monroe said.

"Oh, thanks, that's okay."

"I insist. Someone should enjoy the pool. If you don't have a bathing suit, you know we keep a variety for guests. Everything is in the pool house."

"I actually have a suit in my car, but…"

"Splendid! Stay as long as you like. I'll see you the day after tomorrow, once you've picked up the samples for the gift bags."

"Sounds good. And if you really don't mind, maybe I'll take you up on your offer."

"Of course. Please do."

Monroe's safari-themed pool house featured bamboo floors, brown and green wallpaper, and chocolate-colored wicker furniture. Tash slipped into her apropos leopard-print bikini and gold aviator sunglasses. *Not bad*, she thought, posing in front of the free-standing, full-length mirror. "Wow, look at these suits and sarongs," she whispered, admiring the large rack of designer swimwear carefully arranged for guests. *Wonder how many celebrities have worn these*, she thought, brushing her hands across the garments. *Monroe has some life*. She sprayed sunscreen all over herself and headed outside. Henry was waiting.

"I took the liberty of placing towels on that chaise under the umbrella," he said, pointing. "There's a diet cola on the table and I put several floats in the pool. Please let me know if I can get you anything else."

"Thanks, H. You're the best," she said, patting his back as she passed by.

"You're quite welcome, Miss Daniels."

Tash sat on the edge of the pool, her feet soaking in the warm, aqua water, her eyes focused on the majestic estate. She imagined what it would be like to live there. She always felt for those born in America, there were two versions of the American dream: the worker's version and the dreamer's version. This was the dreamer's version. This was where improbability kissed reality, sparking like a firework and casting an iridescent film over everything it touched. The glistening estate was merely a grand symbol of a dream realized. Tash was captivated. She took her sunglasses off, slid into the pool, and waded over to the bright pink flamingo float. *This is the life*, she thought, hoisting herself up onto the hot plastic bird. *A tequila sunrise would make this moment perfect. I should hit the club tonight, get back into the swing. Maybe Lu's working.*

After floating around for twenty minutes, she was parched and disembarked from her flamingo with a head-first dive. Gently gliding underwater all the way to the stairs, her mind cleared. She sauntered over to the chaise, casually reclined, and sipped her soda. *Too bad I don't have my iPod. I'll just chill for a bit and then head out*, she thought, closing her eyes. *This is so relaxing*, she mused, as she drifted off to sleep.

Soon, Tash was dreaming that she was walking down Abbott Kinney Boulevard in Venice Beach. Although she knew the stores well, they all looked different. Two mannequins in a window slowly began moving their heads toward each other. "This is weird. It's like a Björk video. What's in the next window?" Grass was springing from the floor, working its way up the mannequins' legs. "That's strange." She walked on. There was a large television in the third window, projecting Aidan's face.

"What are you doing, beauty queen?"

"Aidan?" she asked.

"Look everyone, it's my muse," he bellowed.

"Wait, what are you saying?" she pleaded.

She pressed her hands and face against the glass.

"Love you, beauty queen. Gotta go."

"Wait, Aidan!"

Static.

Her heart racing, she continued walking, quickening her pace, but soon feared she was slipping through the ever-widening cracks beneath her feet. She slammed her body against the next store window and caught her breath. Turning her head, she saw her reflection, frightened and undone. There was a Help Wanted sign that read:

Wanted: beauty seekers

Positions to fill: countless

Hours: time is slipping by

"Time is slipping by?" As she said the words aloud, the crack in the cement below her feet widened more. She prepared to leap over it, and then took flight. In midair, her stomach dropped. Tash's body shook violently and she woke up like a bolt.

"Huh," she mumbled, trying to acclimate herself. She sipped her watery cola before noticing the position of the sun. *Shit. I must have been asleep for a while.*

***

Dazed from sitting in rush hour traffic and troubled by her peculiar dream, Tash didn't notice Darrell standing outside her building smoking a cigarette until he called to her.

"Hey there," he said.

"Oh, hey. Did you hit the pier today?" she hollered.

He shook his head. "There's a time to sell and a time to create."

She smiled.

"You know the time to sell, right?" he asked.

She shrugged.

"When the rent's due."

She laughed half-heartedly and waved goodbye.

There's a time to sell and a time to create. Hmm. Bet he never gets creatively blocked. Feeling down, she took a shower and then looked in the mirror, debating whether she had the energy to go clubbing. *I'm spent from the sun,* she concluded before changing into sweats and a tank top. Her laptop sat on her dresser, taunting her. She grabbed it and switched it on. The seconds it took to boot up felt impossibly longer than the seconds before. There was a slowness to time that recalled her dream. *My muse? Is that what he said?* By the time her desktop loaded, she decided that she was too tired to work and flipped it off. *I'm kinda hungry.* She scoured the kitchen for something to eat. Settling on a tub of Campbell's Chicken & Stars soup, she stuck it in the microwave. Soon she was carrying her soup and a Diet Coke to her bedroom where she turned the TV on and slid into bed. She flipped through the stations and landed on *Purple Rain. Ooh good, it just started.* She blew on her soup before eating a spoonful. *Wonder what'll be on after this.*

For the next few weeks, Tash followed the same routine: running errands, working with Monroe, who seemed increasingly tired, swimming and sunning, texting Aidan to avoid FaceTime, staring at her film files without opening them, contemplating going to the clubs, eating soup from a tub, and watching movies. Eventually, she stopped turning on her laptop altogether.

***

Lu and Paisley had become inseparable. They went hiking, spent lazy afternoons at the beach, and strolled around farmer's markets. Paisley hung out at clubs while Lu worked. Every night they went back to Lu's, and every morning they awoke entangled in each other's arms. Paisley invited Lu to meet her friends a couple of times, but Lu cited work as an excuse not to go. One Friday morning before they got out of bed, Paisley asked again.

"So, you're off tomorrow, right?"

"Yeah. What do you have in mind?" Lu asked, sliding her hands down Paisley's torso.

Paisley giggled. "Well, *that* of course, but I was thinking of you coming somewhere with me tomorrow night."

"Where?"

"To a midnight screening of *The Rocky Horror Picture Show* in West Hollywood. It's this thing my friends and I do the first Saturday of every month. It's my only night owl thing, well, before you came along."

"Seriously?" Lu asked.

"You're not a drama nerd or a film geek so you may not get it, but yeah, it's actually really fun. You've seen it before online or something, right?"

"No, never did."

"Seriously?!" Paisley exclaimed, leaning back to register her shock.

"Okay, now I feel lame."

"No, I'm just surprised, that's all. So, you up for it?"

"I guess, sure."

Paisley smiled brightly. "You can dress up, but you don't have to."

"Uh, okay."

"Could you meet me there? I always go early to see my friends and stuff."

"Sure. Maybe I'll ask Tash to come if that's cool. Since you've been occupying all my time, I haven't really talked to her. I feel bad about it. She's having a hard time with the whole Aidan thing, even if she won't admit it," Lu said.

"Definitely. Bring her. It's about time I meet her. I'll leave tickets for you both at the box office. And I was thinking one more thing."

"Oh yeah, what's that?" Lu asked softly, touching the side of her face.

"Maybe after, you could come grab a bite with my friends."

Lu inhaled and looked into Paisley's eyes, her hand still on her face. "Yeah, I can do that."

CHAPTER 9

"It's usually not so tough to find a spot around here," Lu said.

"I'm telling you, my parking karma is totally fucking shot," Tash moaned, as she and Lu drove down the same street for the third time.

"Go down a couple of blocks before you circle this time," Lu suggested.

"Look at how many homeless people there are. Those tents must be crazy hot this time of year," Tash said. "It's really depressing."

"Yeah, it's gotten a lot worse in the past few years."

"Did I ever tell you about Harold, the homeless dude I was kinda friends with in New York?" Tash asked.

"Don't think so."

"Like I brought him coffee and doughnuts sometimes and we'd talk. He hung out in Washington Square Park near my apartment. The NYU kids treated him like crap. Maybe I thought I was better than them. But I probably wasn't."

"What do you mean? What happened to him?" Lu asked.

Tash sighed. "Not sure. I was having a bad day once and I was kind of bitchy to him."

"Nah, not you!" Lu joked.

"Hardy har har. Anyway, I never saw him again. Suddenly, he wasn't there, like he vanished. It bothered me for a long time, wondering what happened to him. And then I started to think about how I called him my friend, but it's not like I invited him over or ever actually helped him get his life together. Maybe I was just nice to him to make myself feel better."

Lu was about to respond when she spotted a driver getting into their car. "Over there," she hollered. Tash pulled up, waiting with her blinker on. The driver of the other car seemed to be in no rush to leave.

"Hurry the fuck up," Tash grumbled.

"Chill, we have time," Lu said, as the car slowly moved out.

Tash pulled into the spot. They hopped out into the steamy night air and started walking toward the theater.

"Thanks for coming with me. I was sort of surprised you wanted to," Lu said.

"Uh, what do I love most in the world?"

"I don't know. Your hair?"

Tash winced. "Very funny."

"Film. You love film."

"Yup. Besides, I haven't gone anywhere except work in weeks. Been hibernating. It's probably good you dragged my ass out." Then Tash looked more carefully at Lu. "What's with the blue jeans and button-down shirt? You look so cleaned up."

"Paisley said to dress up."

"Uh, dumbass, she meant to dress as one of the characters."

"What?"

"Oh my God, I still can't believe you've never seen this before. At a lot of screenings, people dress up like the characters in the film. They even act out certain parts, like jumping up in the aisles and doing this dance, 'The Time Warp.' It's like a whole thing."

Lu shook her head. "Christ."

"It's fun. You'll see."

"Am I too dressed up?" Lu asked.

"Yup, but it's fine. No one who goes to these things is judgmental. They're like a misfit cult or something."

"Be careful what you say. You were pretty into it when I invited you," Lu said with a laugh.

"I'm a film junkie and Rocky Horror has had the longest theatrical run in history. Of course I'm into it. Besides, I want to meet your girl."

"She's not my girl," Lu said, looking down at her feet. "Well, I guess she is, but don't say that kind of stuff in front of her, okay?"

"I thought you were really into her," Tash said.

"I mean, she's amazing. She's such a good person. Too good, you know? I just don't know if I'm ready to do the whole relationship thing."

Tash chuckled. "I thought lesbians were all about the love at first sight, 'let's get a place together' thing."

"I'm not that kind of queer."

Before Tash could respond, they bumped into the end of a long line of people waiting to get into the theater. The line was wrapped around the corner, and most people were dressed in campy makeup, wigs, and costumes.

"This is so weird," Lu whispered.

"Chill, you'll see. But please tell me we're on the list or something," Tash said.

"Yeah, Paisley said to go straight to the box office window."

***

"I don't see her anywhere," Lu said, scanning the crowded theater.

"Relax and sit. We're dead center. She'll find us," Tash said.

The red velvet seat creaked as Lu sat down. "Give me your purse so I can save the seat next to me." Tash handed over her purse and Lu placed it beside her. "So, you've been busy working for Monroe?"

"Yeah, but she's going out of town tomorrow. I'll have a couple of weeks off."

"Cool. Doesn't Aidan's record drop soon?"

Tash thought for a moment. "Wow. Yeah, midnight tomorrow, actually. I've been so preoccupied I lost track."

"Since your boss and your guy are both on the road, why don't you come to the club tomorrow night? Haven't seen you there in a while. The party isn't the same without you. Do it for LA."

Tash giggled. "I haven't really been in the mood, I guess."

"Get back out there. Put on one of your killer outfits and let loose. I'm working the late shift the next couple of nights."

"Damn, you're gonna be dragging."

"I'm almost used to it," Lu joked.

Suddenly, the lights went out. The audience started pounding their feet and cheering.

A woman asked Lu to move the purse so she could sit. When she said it was the last open seat in the theater, Lu begrudgingly gave in.

"I don't understand where Paisley is. It's not like her to flake."

"Don't worry. She must be here. She'll find us after," Tash whispered.

"Listen, think about what I said. You're a club chick. Be who you are. Maybe it feels like A's space, but it isn't."

Tash offered a half-hearted shrug and then whispered, "Yeah, thanks. Now focus. You're gonna love this."

Lu rolled her eyes.

The film began. As an image of red lips appeared on screen, reflecting light onto the faces of the faithful audience, Lu waited in anticipation. When the opening wedding scene began, a troupe of actors ran in from the wings and began acting out the scene in front of the screen.

Tash squeezed Lu's wrist and whispered, "This is the bomb. Some theaters have volunteer casts that act out the whole thing live. Never got to see that before."

Lu smiled and then noticed Paisley among the wedding guests. She was wearing a lavender skirt suit and white hat. In unison with the running film, she caught the wedding bouquet.

Lu whispered, "That's Paisley."

"Oh my God. She's Janet."

Lu shrugged.

Tash leaned closer and whispered, "She's totally making fun of her goody-goody image. Brilliant. Just watch."

Enthralled by what was unfolding, Lu couldn't take her eyes off Paisley.

Soon, Brad and Janet were walking in the rain toward a mysterious castle. With a folded newspaper over her head, perfectly wide-eyed, Paisley mouthed along, "There's a light…"

A smile began to creep onto Lu's face.

When "The Time Warp" started to play, everyone in the theater jumped up to participate. Tash showed Lu how to follow along.

Before long, Paisley was stripped down to her white bra and slip, childlike barrettes still clipped in her hair. Lu's smile brightened. During the climactic sexual liberation scene, when Paisley began throwing her head back and mouthing, "Touch-a, touch-a, touch-a, touch me. I want to be dirty," Lu, utterly mesmerized, smiled so wide it morphed into laughter. In that moment, with the glow of the screen reflecting on her face, Lu gave in to her feelings. She looked at Paisley and the cinematic images projected behind her and had one clear thought: *Damn. I love this girl.*

***

The lights came on and people started making their way out of the theater. Lu checked her phone and saw a text from Paisley:

```
Need to change real quick. Will meet
you in the lobby.
```

Lu and Tash waited as the rest of the audience filed out. Tash, obviously captivated by the building, was looking all around.

"This place is dope. I love these old, restored theaters. There's so much history. This one's super gothic. Imagine the premieres that took place here back in the day. I bet it was raunchy in the eighties."

"Yeah, it's cool." Lu was visibly nervous.

"What's with you?"

"Paisley was really something, huh?"

Tash nodded. "She's hot. And she definitely has a good, ironic sense of herself. I dig her."

"Yeah, me too," Lu said.

Tash smiled. "Lean in."

"I'm kinda getting that message," Lu conceded.

Soon, Paisley and four of her castmates were skipping into the lobby on what one called "a post-show high." After introductions, they walked to a nearby all-night diner. Paisley explained it was their after-show tradition.

At the diner, everyone ordered eggs, pancakes, or pie, except for Lu, who opted for a meatloaf sandwich at everyone's urging. The group of vegetarians was oddly thrilled someone could finally honor Meatloaf's performance in the film. As she bit into the sandwich and gravy dripped on her hand, Lu said she was "glad to sacrifice for the group." After an hour and a half of lively conversation, raucous laughter, and comfort food, Lu sat with her arm around Paisley, her belly and heart both full.

***

"Thanks for driving us, Tash," Lu said as they pulled up to Lu's apartment building. Paisley leaned forward from the backseat to peck Tash on the cheek. "It was great to finally meet you," she said.

"You too," Tash replied.

"Maybe I'll see you at the club tomorrow night."

"Yeah, I'll try," Tash said.

Paisley and Lu hopped out of the car, but Lu leaned back into the open passenger window. "So, you'll come tomorrow night?"

"Probably."

"Okay. Thanks for tonight. It was actually really fun."

"Yeah, your girl is great."

Lu smiled. "Yeah, she is."

CHAPTER 10

"Monroe, is there anything you'd like me to put in the car?" Bill called from the bedroom.

Monroe stared in the bathroom mirror, wondering if the dark circles under her eyes were as pronounced as she feared, or if they were like her heartbeat, louder in her own mind. She took a deep breath before responding, "No thank you, darling. Henry already loaded my small travel bag and my books."

"I need to make a quick call. I'll meet you at the car."

"Be down in a minute."

Even that brief exchange depleted her energy, so she sat perfectly still, taking deep, purposeful breaths. She plucked a tube of concealer off the vanity, rubbed the porcelain-colored goop on her fingertip, and gently dabbed it under each eye. She sat for another moment, vacantly gazing at the mirror before sauntering into her bedroom to fetch her beige Hermès handbag and oversized, black Chanel sunglasses. At the last minute, she rifled through her nightstand and removed an unopened prescription for valium. With the bottle tucked safely in her handbag, Monroe headed out. She stopped at her beloved Warhol, almost involuntarily, and cocked her head as if trying to see the brightly colored image from a new perspective. *Marilyn, I read something you wrote, something about how you felt life coming closer. Had it been further? Had you been removed from your own life? Is that what Mr. Warhol saw? Is that what he was trying to show us?*

Her daydream was interrupted when Bill called from the bottom of the staircase. "We should get on the road before the traffic picks up."

She smiled ever so slightly at the painting, slipped on her sunglasses, and hollered, "Coming, darling."

***

Bill turned north onto the 101, flipping through the stations on the radio.

"Oh, leave that on," Monroe said, as Billie Holiday's voice oozed through the speakers.

"Looks like an easy ride today," he said.

"You should have taken the driver so you could relax."

"It's my only chance to drive. If I had my way, we'd be in one of the convertibles."

"Oh Bill, you know the wind and sun are too much for me."

"That's why I leave one of them at the ranch house. We can just do a short, local drive when we're there. It's an excuse for you to put your hair up in one of those silk scarves I bought you in Paris."

"Mmhmm," Monroe sighed.

"Maybe you should try to take a nap. It's been weeks since you've slept properly. I don't remember you suffering like this since before we got married, after your…" he trailed off.

"Yes, I know."

"Back then, your doctor prescribed something. Maybe…"

Monroe interrupted. "Yes, I already got something, just in case."

"Hopefully you won't need it. A change of scenery will do you good. Riding always knocks you out, and the horses will be happy to see you too."

She turned toward him and smiled faintly. "I think you're right, darling. Perhaps I'll close my eyes for a bit."

"When we get to Ventura, should I stop at that produce stand you like?" Bill asked. "We could get greens for your smoothies and maybe some melon for breakfast."

"All right," she muttered, her eyelids becoming heavier. As Billie Holiday warbled her last note, Monroe shut her eyes.

I should remember to get kale and spinach. Oh, and cucumbers. I always forget the cucumbers. Bill wants melon. Perhaps they'll have nice cantaloupe. He loves cantaloupe. Suspended somewhere between sleeping and waking, her thoughts drifted to the supermarket where she worked at as a teenager. She remembered the day she quit, at the age of sixteen, as if it had just happened.

Her twenty-two-year-old manager, Tom, a tall, skinny man with dark hair and sparse stubble on his short chin, called her over the store intercom.

"Jenny Anne to the stockroom."

She headed straight to the stockroom, glad to have a break from bagging groceries, a job that made time move slower than the little turtles Lauren raced with her brother. Tom was already in the small, dank room, holding a clipboard. A crate of honeydew melons sat atop a stack of boxes.

"These melons need to be shelved," he said.

"Sure thing," she replied, wriggling past him in the cramped space. She placed her hand on a melon when she heard the clipboard drop onto the small table beside them. Suddenly, she felt him standing behind her, not a centimeter separating them.

"Those melons should be ripe," he said, his voice lower than usual.

"Uh huh," she mumbled.

He placed his hand on the melon she was touching, his body now pressed against her.

"You've been here for almost a year, right?" he asked softly. "Feel that melon. When something's ripe, it starts to smell different. When you bite into it, the sweetness drips from your mouth."

Her heart thumping, she said, "I'm all set here. I got it on my own."

"You sure you don't need my help?" he whispered, still pressed firmly against her.

"I'm all set," she replied, trying to control her shaking.

He stepped back. "When you're done with those, you can go on your break."

She inhaled, holding her breath until she was certain he was gone. She shelved all the melons, collected her backpack from her locker, and walked out of the store as if she was taking her break. She never went back, not even to get her last paycheck.

By the time she got home, tears were streaming down her face. She cleaned herself up before her mother got home from work, not wanting to upset her after a long day and afraid she might blame her "attention-getting" appearance for the incident. At dinner, she casually announced she quit her job because it had nothing to do with what she wanted to do in life. For weeks, she and her mother argued about it, her mother insisting "life isn't just made up of things we like." Lauren was the only person she confided in. After that, whenever her mother sent her to the grocery store, she took two buses to go to the store two towns over.

Every night, as she lay in bed counting the Day-Glo shooting stars on her ceiling, she dreamt of a life far away from minimum wage, managers, and buses. Sometimes she'd picture herself on the cover of Vogue and she'd imagine Tom, old and ugly, bagging groceries and looking at stacks of magazines adorned with her face.

***

As they pulled away from the produce stand, Bill turned the radio back on. Sinatra came through the speakers. "Ah, this is perfect for the scenic part of the drive," Bill said.

Monroe smiled. "You're so old-fashioned. I do love that about you."

Bill laughed. "I've been blessed with good taste."

Monroe giggled. "I love the coastal part of the trip." She gazed past Bill, the deep blue water of the Pacific glistening in the sun. "The water in California always sparkles," she said softly.

Bill turned the music up and Monroe watched the water as if it were a film where the past and present met. Her husband provided the soundtrack. Her eyelids once again became heavy, but she fought to keep them open.

It always sparkles, she thought. *I'll never forget the first time I saw the Pacific. Vast and glorious, just like I imagined my future would be.*

She landed in LA with less than a thousand dollars in the bank and everything she owned crammed into two suitcases. She had hustled, mailing her semi-professional headshots to various modeling and talent agencies, the latter offering no response. However, she had meetings arranged with three modeling agencies and was told if she was signed, they would help her get settled and send her on go-sees to clients right away. Confident that she could make big things happen for herself, she ignored her bank balance and hailed a cab at LAX. When the cabdriver asked, "Where to?" she handed him a slip of paper with the address of a cheap motel she had booked. He warned her, "Be careful. That's a rough area."

"That's okay. I won't be there long. Oh, and sir, can you drive by the Pacific? I've never seen it before."

"It's out of your way and will cost you more."

"That's okay. Please take the longer route."

***

When the Prestons arrived at their home away from home, they were promptly greeted by their housekeeper, who ran outside to help them. Bill handed her the cardboard box overflowing with fresh produce.

"Oh my, these berries are beautiful," she said. "I'll get these into the house right away."

"Thank you," Bill said, as he retrieved Monroe's bag from the trunk. "Feeling better? You dozed off in the car."

"Yes, a bit better."

"Shall we head inside?"

Monroe nodded. "I think after we settle in, I'll go to the stables, see the horses. Perhaps I'll go for a short ride."

Monroe changed into her riding clothes in her bedroom. She noticed the small, framed photograph of her mother on her dresser. Her mother was young and uncharacteristically wearing a party dress. It was Monroe's favorite photo. She picked it up and smiled. "Oh Mama, you were beautiful. Strange how you spent your life making party dresses for other women, but never for yourself. You never did care much for fancy clothes or makeup, but you didn't need any of that. I'm sorry I thought you were plain or simple. You weren't, were you?"

She gently placed the frame back on the dresser and sat on the edge of the bed, thinking about the day she called her mother boasting she'd been signed to a modeling agency.

"Mama, I don't understand why you aren't more excited."

"I told you, I'm happy for you if this is what you want."

"They set me up with an apartment with a bunch of other girls. They think I'd be good at print work, and I have go-sees all week."

"Go...?"

"Go-sees, Mama. They're like auditions."

"The thought of you parading around for them and being judged – judged on your God-given body..."

Monroe rolled her eyes. "It's not like that, not really. Besides, if I book some jobs, I'll be able to take another stab at talent agencies, maybe try my hand at acting."

"I just don't know how anyone could be happy like that, being rejected all the time."

"Mama, did you ever think that some people just are happy, and even if they're not, they're trying to be?" After a long silence, Monroe changed the subject. "What about you, Mama?"

"Oh, well, I'm fine. I'm the same."

"How's work?"

"The same as always."

"Have you gone to play cards at Elaine's?"

"I've been too tired." She paused for a moment. "Jenny Anne, we should hang up. This call will be very expensive for you."

"Maybe someday we won't have to worry about that. I'll call you next week."

"Call after seven when it's less expensive."

"Yes, Mama."

"And Jenny Anne, if you're happy, *truly* happy, that's all a person can hope for, I suppose."

"I'll call next week. Wish me luck. Bye, Mama."

All these years later, Monroe could recall every detail of that conversation. *Was dressmaking in that small town really your ideal life? I remember the stacks of unpaid bills, and you, sitting alone every night, eating reheated casserole and watching game shows. Weekends spent cleaning the house or doing odd jobs. Oh, I wish I knew what your dreams had been. You must have had some, even if you held onto them tightly. Or was it that you let them go too easily?* Her thoughts shifted to her mother's words about happiness: "If you're happy, *truly* happy, that's all a person can hope for." She began to wonder about her tone. She tried to remember how she sounded. *Were you mournful? Was I too preoccupied to truly hear you? Oh Mama, were you ever happy? If you were, when did your happiness end? When did life slip farther away?*

***

Luke, the stablehand, had prepared Monroe's favorite horse, Captain, in case she wanted to go for a ride. As she mounted the beautiful animal, his coat the color of dark chocolate with creamy white splotches along his gait, she whispered, "Oh Captain, how I've missed you."

"I took him out for a walk so he's ready for whatever you have in mind. I'll be here when you get back," Luke said.

Monroe nodded and then gently pressed on her horse. He began walking. There was little that brought Monroe the peace and joy she felt with her horses. She'd spent twenty-five years searching for meaning in religion, spirituality, astrology, mythology, self-help, and countless fads that had quickly come and gone, but she felt most centered when she was riding. It cleared her mind. But today, she couldn't focus on the horse, the breeze, or the sunshine. She couldn't quiet her mind. She began to wonder why she felt out of sorts these past few weeks, unsettled, and outside of the moment.

Bill adores me. Our lives are perfect. I have more freedom and glamour than I ever could have envisioned. What's wrong with me? Her mother's words came barreling into her mind. *"Glamour alone isn't a goal. It isn't a life."* She remembered when she called her mother to announce her engagement and the argument that ensued.

"Why are you always so negative? You're never happy for me."

"That isn't true. I just don't want to see you throw your life away. You're too young, you barely know him, and my God, Jenny Anne, he's too old for you."

"Stop being so provincial. He's not old, he's accomplished."

"And what will you accomplish in your life?"

"Do you know how many girls would kill to marry someone like Bill? Do you know how lucky I am?"

"You need time to find out who you are and what you can do for yourself. There will always be men who want to take care of a girl as pretty as you."

"Then why were you alone your whole life?" she shrieked. "Working till your fingers were raw, sitting alone at home and crying at night. Don't you think I heard you, whimpering, crying yourself to sleep?"

No response. When what seemed like an eternity had passed, Monroe softened her voice. "I'm sorry, Mama. You know I'm grateful for everything you did for me. I just want you to be happy for me. We're different, that's all."

"Jenny Anne, I hope you find what you're looking for. Call me next week."

"Bill is gonna buy your airline ticket for the wedding. He'll take care of everything. Don't forget, it's just a couple of months away."

"I'll talk to you next week."

"Bye, Mama."

Embarrassed by what she had said and preoccupied with planning a whirlwind wedding, she didn't call her mother for three weeks. When they finally spoke, her mother was quieter than usual, distant. Things that would usually provoke an argument got no reaction at all. Her mother's response to everything was, "that's nice," which was how she always spoke to others, but never to Monroe. Feeling guilty, Monroe assumed her change in demeanor was because of the hurtful words she had spoken weeks earlier.

Three days later, a police officer called to inform her that her mother had been killed in a car accident. Her car veered off the road, slamming into a tree. Monroe was devastated. Instead of flying her mother out to California, Monroe and Bill flew in for the funeral. After the service, she hosted mourners in her mother's home. The next-door neighbor, Elaine, walked over and hugged Monroe tightly. Elaine and her mother sometimes stopped at each other's homes for coffee, to play cards, or with a bowl of soup if one or the other was sick.

"I'm just so sorry, Jenny Anne. I always knew of your mother's troubles, but if I had thought…"

Monroe's eyes widened. "What are you saying, Elaine? It was a car accident."

Elaine took Monroe's hands. "It was a clear night and there were no skid marks. No other cars. You've always been such a firecracker that you kept her going, kept the flicker of fight alive in her. But once you were grown… I'm sure you knew… she always had such a sadness about her. She…"

Monroe squeezed her hands and released. "Thank you for coming."

Monroe didn't sleep for weeks. Bill suggested postponing the wedding, but she refused, saying, "Life is too short." He couldn't argue.

As she rode her horse, the afternoon sun beating on her face, she thought about every word her mother spoke in those final phone calls, trying to compare them to all the words she had spoken before. The words were like an avalanche threatening to overtake her mind. She squeezed her calves and heels and her horse began to gallop. *"You need to find out who you are. Glamour alone isn't a goal. Fancy dresses and parties don't make people happy. Life will disappoint you. You look like tinsel sparkling under twinkly lights."* Desperate to outrun the avalanche, she applied more pressure and screamed, "Go, Captain." He began galloping at full speed, the wind pushing against her skin, pushing against the words.

CHAPTER 11

Tash was walking home from her favorite neighborhood boutique, swinging her shopping bag back and forth, when her phone rang. She flipped her sunglasses onto the top of her head and smiled as Lu's name flashed on the screen.

"Hey baby, what's up?"

"Just checking to see if you're comin' tonight."

"As a matter of fact, I just bought the fiercest little dress."

Lu chuckled. "You go, girl."

"Since when did you get so formal? Why not text?" Tash queried.

"Didn't want you to dodge me."

"As iiiiiif," Tash said, exaggerating the word.

"Glad to hear you're back to your old smart ass, it-girl self."

"Well, someone has to save the LA club scene from the monotony of the reality star brigade and their Z-list groupies."

"That's the spirit!" Lu exclaimed.

"I'll see you tonight. Ciao, baby."

"Ciao."

***

With her favorite eighties playlist blaring and a towel wrapped around her freshly showered body, Tash applied a final coat of hot pink lipstick. She stepped back and puckered her lips, blowing her reflection a kiss. *I need some extra pizazz*, she mused, adding a streak of silver glitter eyeliner above her signature black liquid liner. She batted her long, false eyelashes. *I've still got it.*

The Smiths' "How Soon Is Now" swirled in the air as she strutted into her bedroom and plucked the last couple of pieces of popcorn from the microwave bag on her nightstand, eating them one by one. Her new, sparkling silver dress was hanging on the back of the door. She slipped the slinky mini on, placing the spaghetti straps on her freckled shoulders. *Where are my strappy silver heels?* she wondered, scouring her closet. "Ah, you were hiding! Guess I haven't worn you in a while."

Sitting on the edge of her bed to buckle her shoe straps, she glanced up and saw the picture she and Aidan took on their first day in LA. Hair in a ponytail and makeup-free, she had tried to shield her face, but Aidan insisted on capturing the start of their adventure together. It was the only picture she'd ever put in a frame. She paused to examine their goofy smiles, then grabbed her purse and headed out.

***

Tash's mood had plummeted by the fifth time she passed the club, searching for a parking space. Circling the block in larger and larger loops felt like a less-than-subtle metaphor for her life. She feared her luck had simply run out. What was once within reach felt further and further away. Everything had always fallen neatly into place, but now nothing quite fit. Even her shoes felt too tight. Lost in her own troubles, she barely noticed the people camping out merely blocks away from the club. When they eventually caught her eye, she realized they were getting closer each month: the truth encroaching on the lie. *Must be more of them. Fuck, it's sad. It's like the fires springing up in the canyons, getting harder to control, harder to keep at bay. They're warnings that there's no such place as paradise, because there's always a shadow side. People here like everything to be airbrushed. They like their pretty pictures. Everything is filtered.* As a yellow Aston Martin zoomed past her, likely carrying fellow club-goers, she was confronted with multiple realities. Her complicated relationship with LA blurred at the intersection of her waning dreams and the stark reality that her life was indeed privileged.

By the time she found a parking spot, she was vacillating between rage and despair, but no longer sure why. Determined to shake it off and have a fabulous night, she turned her attention forward, ignoring everything in the periphery.

Reinvigorated, she breezed past the line of beautiful people. The bouncer ushered her over and unlatched the rope. As she passed through, he called, "How's A? You think he'll ever come back?" Her body clenched, but she turned, smiled at him with a shrug, and then walked into the packed club.

Tash wriggled her way through the crowd, slowly making her way to the bar. She stood for a couple of minutes before Leo handed her a tequila sunrise.

"You're slipping! Your arm's usually out before I make it over," she hollered over the noise.

"I know. Epic fail. Wasn't expecting to see you; you've been MIA. We all figured you went on tour with A after all."

"Nope. Just been busy. But I'm back," she said.

"And hotter than ever, but don't tell your man I said that."

She winked at him and held up her glass. "Cheers," she said, taking a gulp.

Leaning against the bar and steadily sipping her drink, Tash surveyed the room. It was full of the usual suspects. Lu was on the deejay platform, flaunting her favorite vintage David Bowie T-shirt and black leather pants as she rocked her sound. Paisley was holding her own on the dance floor. They were exchanging looks. *Wow, never thought I'd see the day. Lu's totally in love. It's great.* Just then, Lu glanced over, smiled brightly, and cocked her head. Tash held up her arm to say hi in return. Several people asked her to dance and offered to buy her drinks. Despite relishing the attention, she declined, gesturing to the one in her hand. Paisley came over and they chatted for a while. As Tash was finishing her second drink, a tall guy with a chiseled face and midnight-black hair sidled up to her.

"You're the most drop-dead beautiful woman here tonight. You know that, right?" he asked in a sexy English accent.

"That's quite the line," she said.

"Ah, I'm gutted," he said, grabbing his chest. "I did want to impress you, but I can tell that's no easy task."

The corners of her mouth turned up in an almost imperceptible smile.

"Take pity on me and have a dance?" he asked.

She gave him the once-over, took the last sip of her drink, and nodded. With electro-techno beats guiding the way, they made their way onto the dance floor. Tash danced freely, happily losing herself in the moment. After fifteen minutes, her dance partner leaned in and said, "By the way, my name is Liam."

"I'm Tash."

"Oh, I know who you are," he shouted over the music.

Puzzled, she leaned in closer. "What do you mean?"

"My friends told me you're A-A-Aidan's muse. Don't worry, I know you're taken. I'm a musician and I was just hoping some of that good luck might rub off on me."

Repelled, she stepped back. Bodies whirled all around her, but Tash was perfectly still.

"Oh, I'm sorry. I didn't mean to offend you," Liam said.

"No problem. I need a break. See ya," she said, as she walked away.

His muse? Just like that fucking dream. Is that how people fucking see me now? Her internal rant continued all the way to the restroom where she intended to regroup. She tried to calm down, but her mind was flooded with warring images of herself – those projected from others were indecipherable from her own. She wanted to be carefree and strong, but another part of her wanted to run home and crawl into bed. *Fuck that. And fuck Aidan for putting me in this situation. I should be able to have a good fucking time.*

Determined to "have fun" no matter what, she made a beeline for the bar and ordered a third drink. Halfway through her drink, Texas appeared.

"Hey there, pretty lady," he said, running his fingers through his shaggy blonde hair.

"Hey, Texas. How ya been?"

"Can't complain, can't complain. Missing you, of course. Where you been hiding out?"

"Not hiding, just busy."

"Well, I sure am glad you're here tonight. This place is stuffed to the gills with rich kids blowing their trust funds."

"Yeah, nothing stays cool around here for long," Tash groaned.

"I don't want your boyfriend to kick my ass, but I must say, holy smokes you're looking mighty fine."

"Well he's not around these days, so I wouldn't worry about it."

"In that case, you want to finally grace me with your presence on the dance floor?"

Just as she was about to respond, Lu announced another deejay was taking over while she took a short break.

"Sorry, Texas. My friend is coming over. Later, okay?"

"Sure thing, pretty lady. Find me."

Tash watched as he walked away. Lu leapt off the platform, said something to Paisley, and then made her way to the bar.

"Damn, girl! You weren't kidding. You look amazing," Lu said.

"Thanks, baby. You're looking like a total boss, as usual."

Lu shrugged sarcastically. "Well, you know, I gotta represent. You having a good time?"

"Trying," Tash said. She inhaled deeply, but before she could elaborate, the deejay made an announcement, and they both turned to listen.

"Hey everyone! It's midnight, and that means our very own A-A-Aidan's album has dropped." Thunderous applause. He continued, "This is my mix of our boy's single. To your feet, LA!"

Aidan's music swelled and the club was electric. Lu slowly turned to Tash.

"Well, bottoms up, baby," Tash said, raising her drink and downing what was left.

"Hey, you. Take it easy or I'll have to carry you home. My place isn't big enough for three."

"Goddamn it," Tash muttered.

"I was just teasing," Lu said.

"No, it's not that. I'm so stupid, I fucking drove here. It was force of habit, I guess. I always drive and then Aidan drives us home. You know he's a straight edge."

"How many have you had?" Lu asked.

"A few," she replied, playing with the straw in her empty glass.

"Leave your car and Paisley and I will drive you. We'll get your car tomorrow."

"I don't wanna stay all night," Tash whined.

"So Uber it. Paisley will take you to get your car tomorrow."

"Yeah, I guess that will work. Thanks," Tash mumbled.

"Listen, I gotta go to the bathroom and see Paisley before I jump back up there. Promise you won't drive?"

"Scout's honor," Tash said, doing the sign of the cross over her chest.

"Uh, yeah, that's so not from the Scouts. Definitely don't drive."

Tash smiled. "I promise. Go have a good set. Big shoes to fill," she slurred.

Lu winced. "See ya, babe."

"Later."

***

Two hours and two more drinks later, Tash was dancing with Texas when she began to lose her balance, falling into him with increasing regularity.

"Well there, pretty lady. Maybe you need a little break," he said.

"Yeah, maybe I do," she replied.

She tottered over to the bar, occasionally stumbling onto him. He lent a hand as needed. Paisley spotted Tash's inebriated stumbles and came over.

"Tash, do you want me to call an Uber for you?"

"I don't want to leave my car here. Can't get another ticket," she slurred.

"I only had one drink, hours ago. I can drive you in your car if you want," Texas said.

"How will you get home?" Tash asked.

"Uber. No difference to me if it's from here or your place."

"Paisley, I'm gonna go with my good friend Texas, here. We go way back," she said, patting his chest.

"Okay, drink a glass of water and take something for your head when you get home," Paisley said.

Tash nodded, grabbed Texas by the arm, and they headed out into the night.

***

A few minutes later, Paisley was hanging out on the deejay platform with Lu. Lu leaned over and asked, "I saw Tash leave. Did you get her a car?"

"Her friend offered to drive her."

"What friend?"

"Some guy, Texas. She said they're good friends."

Lu shook her head. "He's just a dude that has a monster crush on her."

"Oh my God, is she unsafe?" Paisley asked in a panic.

"Probably only from herself. Oh Tash, what are you doing?" she mumbled.

***

The task of finding Tash's car wasn't made any easier by her poor memory or the fact that she was having trouble balancing in her heels. When they eventually got in the car, Texas asked for her address, which she was miraculously able to communicate along with directions. He opened the windows and she complained, "My hair's gonna get all messed up."

"I think the fresh air will do ya some good," he replied. "How about some tunes?"

"Okay," she said.

He turned the music on and the sounds of the eighties came storming through the speakers. He lowered the volume and said, "Dig the throwback tunes."

"Yeah, me too, or I used to," she mumbled.

"Something bothering you, pretty lady? I got the feeling you were maybe trying to escape a little tonight."

Tash sighed. "Let me ask you something, Texas. Why'd you come to LA?"

"Came to sunny Los Angeles to get away from my family. Woulda gone clear across the country, but I love the warm weather. The big ole Pacific beckoned. Figured I'd take up surfin'."

"You an actor or something?"

"No way. I work at a Mexican restaurant. Saving for a food truck with one of my buddies."

"Wow, Texas. You know, you may be the perfect guy. You're the only person I know who's not here for the bullshit."

"There's no bullshit about you either, I'd reckon."

"Ha! You'd be wrong."

"Havin' a dream don't make it bullshit. Like my food truck. It may not happen, but ain't nothin' wrong with working for it."

"Hmm. Yeah, I guess," she mumbled.

When they arrived at Tash's apartment building, Texas parked the car and they both got out. He handed her the keys.

"Thanks, Texas. You're a nice guy. Such a nice guy," she said, nearly falling onto him. "And you're so good looking. Have I told you that?" she asked.

He blushed and cocked his head. "Can you make it into your apartment?" he asked.

"You've been flirting with me for ages."

"Uh, yes I have. Pretty hard not to. You seen yourself?"

Tash smiled. "That's just what I mean. You always make me feel good. But..."

"But you're definitely drunk and I'm pretty sure you still have a boyfriend. So, if you're okay to make it in, I'm gonna keep on being a nice guy, even though I'll kick myself tomorrow."

She gave him a long look, smiled, and said, "See ya, Texas."

"See ya, pretty lady."

A few minutes later, Tash finally stumbled into her apartment. Dropping her keys on the floor beside the entry table, she made her way to her bedroom. She plopped onto her bed, unbuckled her shoes, and flicked them off. Her feet were throbbing. She took off her dress and slipped on a tank top she found on the floor. *I need to lie down, but if I fall asleep with all this crap on my face, I'll regret it.* Resisting the urge to fall over on the bed, she forced herself to the bathroom. *Music. I need music so I won't pass out.* She flipped her eighties playlist back on, and Duran Duran's "Save a Prayer" filled the room. She listened to the words, staring at her reflection, and thinking about how shamelessly she flirted with Texas. Smeared eyeliner, sweat marks on her face, and a pit in her stomach were all reminders that she had nearly fallen to a new low. She pulled off her false eyelashes and took a long, hard look in the mirror. *I can't believe I came home with Texas. What the fuck was I thinking? If he wasn't such a stand-up guy, what would have happened? I'm such an asshole sometimes. And Aidan. Fucking Aidan. He put up with so much shit with me when we first hooked up. He deserves better. I'm not good enough for him.* As she looked at herself with disdain, her eyes began to well up and tears flowed down her face. She just stood there, drunk and crying. Finally able to catch her breath, she washed her face and raised her gaze to the mirror, patting herself dry. Puffy eyes, freckled skin, and regret stared back at her. She dropped the towel on the floor, shuffled into her bedroom, and collapsed into the bed. She grabbed Aidan's pillow and clenched it tightly until she fell asleep.

CHAPTER 12

Tash woke up late morning, her mouth dry and head throbbing. She grumbled as she opened her eyes, the light piercing her brain. In desperate need of Advil, she dragged herself out of bed and stumbled to the bathroom. Glimpsing herself in the mirror, she recoiled, all the night's foibles etched on her bloodshot eyes and puffy face. She opened the medicine cabinet, retrieved the bottle of Advil, and popped four into her mouth. She turned on the faucet, cupped her hands to collect some water, and then threw back the pills in one gulp. With the medicine cabinet still flung open and pill bottle on the sink, she stumbled back to bed. *Sleep. Please let me fall back asleep until my headache is gone.* Despite the sharp pain emanating from her temples, deep exhaustion won out and she drifted back to sleep.

Tash opened her eyes again at noon, grateful to find that her headache had abated. She wanted to go back to sleep to avoid facing the day for as long as possible, but her stomach growled and she realized she was too hungry to sleep. She got out of bed and lumbered to the kitchen. Aidan's box of Lucky Charms was on the top of the refrigerator. She grabbed the box, stuck her hand in to scoop out some cereal, and hopped onto the counter. Munching on the sweet morsels, she pictured Aidan, standing in his boxers, pouring cereal into a bowl, and then grabbing a fistful to eat dry. Her eyes welled with tears. "No Tash, not again. Not now," she said, wiping her eyes. She finished the cereal, hopped down, and tossed the box in the recycling bin. "Pull yourself together and just do it for him," she whispered. "He can't see me like this. I can't fuck things up for him. Don't be selfish, Tash. Not to him."

She walked into the bedroom, sat on the edge of her bed, and reached for her phone on the nightstand. With the phone gripped tightly in her hands, she took a deep breath, and then, feeling together, called Aidan.

"Hey, beauty queen!" he said.

"Hey, superstar. Congratulations! I can't believe your record is out."

"Yeah, me neither."

"How do you feel?"

"Well, I'm trying to be chill about it with everyone else, but between us, I'm pretty pumped."

"You should be. It's freaking awesome," she said, pausing for a moment before adding, "I'm so proud of you. I really am." As she said these words, she knew she meant them and she felt a twinge of relief.

"Thanks. You know, it goes both ways."

His words hit Tash like a dagger to the heart. She slumped over and inhaled deeply, intent on holding it together. Eventually, Aidan filled the silence.

"I wish you would have FaceTimed so I could see your gorgeous face."

"Believe me, I'm sparing you. Partied a little too hard last night."

"Ah."

"They gave you a huge shout-out at the club. Everyone's really happy for you."

"That's sweet. Glad to hear you went out. From your texts, I get the feeling you've been laying low. You getting any work done?"

"Not really, but I will. You know how tricky inspiration can be."

"Sure do. That's why we can't wait for the muses to visit, we have to chase them."

Hearing those words, Tash couldn't keep the tears back any longer. She sniffled a bit and softly said, "Yeah, I know. I will."

"Are you okay?" he asked.

"Uh huh."

"Really? Because I have no interest in moving backward."

She sighed. "You know I can't keep things from you. I did something kind of stupid last night and I feel like crap."

"How stupid?" he asked, his tone sharper. "Something that can't be undone?"

"No, I stopped myself because," she hesitated, searching for the words before concluding, "because that's not who I want to be."

"Then let it go. We all screw up, but we can't let our mistakes define who we are. Focus on who you are today. Today is what you have."

Tash smiled, wiping the tears from her cheeks.

"I'm pretty lucky to have you," she said.

"You are," he said with a laugh. "Get out in the LA sunshine today. Hit the Getty or the beach."

"Yeah, that's probably a good idea."

"So, how's everything else? Who was spinning at the club last night?"

"Lu, and oh my God, she's totally head over heels. Remember that chick, Paisley, I told you she was sleeping with? Well, they're going strong and I've never seen Lu like this before. I think this might be it for her, although she'd never admit it."

Tash and Aidan continued talking for ten minutes. After they hung up, Tash jumped in the shower, determined to wash away the last night, the last few weeks, and the last residue of who she used to be.

***

"Rise and shine," Lu said, gently stroking Paisley's arm. "I made you breakfast in bed."

"What?" Paisley mumbled, as she opened her eyes.

"I made you breakfast in bed," Lu repeated. "Well, I guess it's more like brunch in bed. It's almost one o'clock."

"Yeah, but the sun was up by the time we went to sleep," Paisley countered, slowly sitting up with a yawn. "How long have you been up?"

"Hours. Couldn't sleep," Lu said as she placed a tray in front of Paisley.

"Uh, yeah, I see that. I can't believe you made me breakfast."

"It's nothing fancy, just oatmeal with strawberries and coffee," Lu said.

"It's perfect. Thank you," Paisley said, taking a sip of coffee.

Lu smiled.

"Why couldn't you sleep? Are you worried about Tash?"

"She's having a really tough time. That's what last night was about."

"Have you heard from her?" Paisley asked, taking a bite of oatmeal.

Lu shook her head. "She'll text me when she's ready. I don't want to push her. We have an unspoken understanding."

Paisley looked at Lu, wide eyed. "Is it all about missing her boyfriend?"

"It's about her feeling like he's on a rocket to the stars and she's stuck on the ground. They actually moved here for her, so she could break into filmmaking. She's faced a lot of roadblocks, a lot of disappointments, and a lot of bullshit, you know? And suddenly, out of nowhere, he's catapulted into the stratosphere and he wasn't even trying." She paused before adding, "And she feels guilty."

Paisley furrowed her brow.

"She feels guilty because she knows she should support him, but the truth is that a part of her resents his success."

"And what about you?" Paisley asked.

"What about me?" Lu replied.

"Is it hard for you?"

"I mean, if I'm really honest, yeah. Aidan is the nicest guy in the world, truly, and he's big time talented. Don't get me wrong – I'm happy for him. But I've been here a lot longer and it's frustrating because as a woman on the circuit, these things just don't happen. Like, *never*. Guys see talent in other guys. They see them as their buddies and they want to go on the road with them. There's no fairness in it, and that always gets to me. And it's not like that kind of success is even my dream; I really just love the music. But it's tough knowing it could never be me."

"I'm sorry," Paisley said.

"Don't be. It's all good. I've just gotta keep reminding myself that the music is what matters."

Just then, Lu's phone beeped. She grabbed it to see a message from Tash, which she read out loud.

```
Hey. I'm fine. Texas was a perfect
gentleman. Sorry if I worried you.
```

"I'm so relieved. I would have felt awful if something happened to her," Paisley said.

"Me too."

Paisley ate a heaping spoonful of oatmeal with a slice of strawberry. "Mmm. This is so good. How come you're so sweet?"

"I'm not. I guess you bring out the best in me."

***

Tash walked along the beach, holding her flip flops as the water rushed over her feet. Looking across the vast cobalt sea, a sense of abundance began to take hold. Mesmerized by the water, she walked farther than planned and soon found herself at the Santa Monica Pier. *Well, why not*, she thought, deciding to take a stroll down the pier.

Children holding soft-serve ice cream cones that melted down their arms walked past her, couples took photographs with selfie sticks, and the famous Ferris wheel slowly spun against the cloudless sky. Craving something sweet, she bought pink cotton candy, indulging in a few sugary bites before tossing it. After a caricaturist tried to convince her to have her portrait done, she decided she'd had enough of the boardwalk. She turned to leave and saw Darrell sitting on a stool with a small painting at his feet, his dreads pulled back in an elastic.

"Hey, Darrell. How's it going?"

"Can't complain."

Tash picked up the painting of a woman's face painted in shades of blue; her eyes were haunting. It was reminiscent of a Picasso and Modigliani hybrid. "Nice work."

"Thanks. Sold a few other small ones today. Funny how the same painting that sells for thousands in a gallery is only worth about sixty bucks on the street." He chuckled. "I'm thinking about calling it a day, it's pretty hot in the sun," he said, beads of sweat dripping down his face.

"Can I give you a ride? My car is a few blocks down."

"That would be great. Thank you."

Darrell folded the legs on his stool, picked up his painting, and they headed home. During the ride, he asked about her work and Tash told him about her short film. As a fellow artist, and one who'd been working at it a bit longer, she realized he might have valuable insights and could help her brainstorm.

"I think I got distracted by the Hollywood thing and how people play the game. Even when I was taking classes, if you didn't follow a certain path, the professors wouldn't throw their weight behind you and you couldn't get into the festivals. My work is artistic," she explained. "A gallery was interested in screening my film, but I blew them off. I was stupid."

"Which gallery?" he asked.

"Patty Price's gallery down on…"

He cut her off. "I know the place. Patty is cool. You should stop by and see if she's still interested."

"Yeah, maybe," Tash said. "You know of any other good galleries?"

"When I first came here, I checked them all out. The scene here didn't exactly welcome me. It was happening for me in New York; I was a part of two group shows in SoHo, and there was this art dealer who hooked me up with high-end clients. Hoped it would translate here, but LA is a fickle place."

"Tell me about it. Fuck. Why'd you leave New York? Sounds like you had it made."

Darrell laughed. "Life happens, you know? Choices have to be made. Come to my place and I'll show you my work."

"Sure," Tash said.

When they arrived at their building, Tash followed Darrell into his apartment, a spacious studio that smelled like turpentine and was overflowing with paintings. Every inch of wall space was covered, and stacks of canvases lined the perimeter of the room. Darrell's life clearly revolved around his art. Half the paintings were of the same subject: a forlorn, dark-haired woman with haunting eyes. Tash stood before one piece, studying it.

"That's Sara, my girlfriend," Darrell said.

"Oh, I didn't know…"

"She's the reason I'm in LA. We lived together in New York for three years. She's a poet. We had wonderful conversations about art, philosophy, religion, all the big ideas, while we worked. I did most of the talking, but she would listen to me, sometimes for hours, encouraging me to go on. She was always quiet, but then one day, her quietness seemed to take hold, like she retreated into herself. Soon she was completely mute and it was as if her beautiful eyes had filmed over."

"Oh my God," Tash mumbled.

"We tried different medications. Nothing worked. I think that shit made her worse. She was from California and I thought the warm weather might help."

"Did it?"

"When her parents saw how bad she was doing, they had her committed to an institution. I'm not even allowed to see her. They blame me for everything."

"That's awful. I'm so sorry," Tash said. "Can I ask why you didn't move back to New York, if it was better for your career?"

"When she's released, I need to be here. This was our last home together."

"How long has it been?"

"Five years. But she'll come back, one day, when she's ready. She'll come back to herself and back to me. I kinda think she's taking a time out from the noise and composing a really long poem. And I'm lucky – I have my art to keep me busy until she's ready to share her beautiful voice again."

Tash smiled.

They said goodbye and Tash headed to her apartment. She grabbed her laptop and plopped onto the bed. She hovered the mouse over the link to her film and clicked on it. For the first time in a long time, she watched her own film.

CHAPTER 13

The day after watching her film, Tash woke up with a fire in her belly. *Be fucking brave*, she told herself. She made a pot of coffee and began an online search for art galleries in Los Angeles, San Francisco, and New York. She decided to start with the local galleries. Adept at using her charisma as currency, she figured her chances were better if she could pitch her case in person.

She visited every gallery and artist cooperative on the list. Some gallerists shooed her off and said that they don't accept "unsolicited works," others said they weren't interested in film work, and some claimed their calendars were booked for years. A couple agreed to watch her film and "let her know." Tired but determined, she sat in her car outside of the last place on her LA list: the Patty Price Gallery. Tash started biting her nails, desperately trying to muster the courage to face Patty, the one gallerist who had loved *Pop Candy*, and the one who Tash had naively blown off. *Be brave. Be fucking brave*, she told herself as she hopped out of the car.

She walked into the gallery. It was her favorite space in LA, with dark wood floors, high ceilings with exposed pipes, and white walls meticulously displaying large, abstract artworks. Tash felt it was the only gallery in LA that had the "it factor" that the New York scene possessed in spades. A young woman with short brown hair was sitting at the desk. Tash walked right over, shoulders back and head high.

"Hi. My name is Tash Daniels and I met with Ms. Price about a year ago. She was interested in showing my short film. I was hoping she might consider it again. Can I leave a message for her?" she asked, handing her a one-page resume.

A voice from behind called, "That won't be necessary."

Tash turned to see none other than Patty Price walking toward her, with her signature dark-rimmed glasses, red lipstick, and perfectly pin-straight, brown bob.

"Patty, it's wonderful to see you. I don't know if you remember me, but my name is Tash Daniels and…"

Patty cut her off. "I remember. You had a film. Seems like forever ago. You know how quickly the art world moves."

"Uh, yes, I do. Listen Patty, I want to apologize for not taking you up on your generous offer to screen the film. At the time…"

Patty put her hand up. "No need to explain. It wasn't right for you. It's your art. I get it."

"Well, that's the thing. I've reconsidered and I was wondering if you might be willing to give me another chance. If you'd just watch it again…"

"I'm booked solid for the next two years. We have your information on file. Thanks for stopping by." Patty abruptly turned to her assistant and began talking.

Tash quietly said, "Thank you," and left.

Although disappointed, Tash kept her spirits up. *Nothing ventured, nothing gained. Be brave.* She also knew that while many people could open or close doors, she was the architect of her own life. Her art and her happiness were in her hands. The weight of that responsibility finally felt like something she could handle, and for the first time, she embraced it.

The next day, she called all the out-of-town galleries on her list. Monroe texted that she decided to extend her trip, so Tash spent the next three weeks making lists of galleries in other cities, researching funding opportunities, and writing. Not quite ready to write her full-length script, she played with ideas. It was thrilling to be back in the creative zone, both planning and experimenting, finally working toward something. Most days she'd forget to eat until her stomach started grumbling in the late afternoon.

The day before Tash's birthday, Monroe returned. Tash stopped by to review final details for the upcoming studio anniversary party. When Tash met her poolside, she noticed Monroe looked run down. They discussed party details, but as their meeting wrapped up, Tash felt compelled to express her concern.

"Are you feeling okay? You look a little tired," Tash remarked.

"Oh, you're sweet to ask. I haven't been sleeping well, but I'm fine."

Monroe quickly changed the subject, giving Tash a pair of gold earrings from Tiffany's and the next two days off to celebrate her birthday. Tash beamed at the sight of the earrings, thanking her profusely.

"It's my pleasure. Wear them well."

"If that's all," Tash said, standing up.

Monroe smiled. "Oh, before you go, I wanted to remind you to pick up the silver pens from the engraver by the end of the day, for the studio party gift bags."

"No problem. I'm heading home to do a few things, but I'll get there before they close."

Tash picked up her Tiffany's gift bag and turned back to Monroe. "Are you sure you're okay?"

"Nothing a little sunshine and sleep can't fix," Monroe said. "Maybe I'll do a face mask. That always helps."

Tash smiled. "Go for it."

***

Running late to make it to the engravers, Tash was frantically searching for her keys when her phone rang. "Fuck, I don't have time for this," she grumbled, but looked to see who was calling anyway. It was a local number that she didn't recognize. Thinking it might be the engraver or one of the other vendors for Monroe's upcoming party, she answered.

"Hello, this is Tash."

"Tash, Patty Price here."

"Oh, hi Patty," Tash said, her heart racing.

"Listen, I'll cut to it. You've probably seen that story on the news about the English video artist arrested for child porn."

"Uh…"

"Well, he was supposed to be a part of a group show starting in two weeks. Apparently, his love for video production was more varied than any of us knew."

"Wow, Patty. That's awful."

"Yeah, well it worked out for you. We were going to show one of his short films in our media room. Now there's a slot open. I know

I wasn't that receptive when you came by, but your work would fit right in. Truth is, I love your film, have since you first showed it to me. Talent is what matters. And you had the chutzpah to come back here. I figure women like us should stick together."

"Thank you. I don't know what to say."

"Say yes. I'm in a rush, dealing with the nightmare of redoing all the signage, flyers, and media announcements."

"Yes. Of course. Thank you."

"My assistant will email you the details. Make sure you're on time for setup, I don't want any problems. And spread the word about the show."

"Okay. And Patty, really, thank you for this."

Tash hung up the phone and jumped up and down. *Did that just happen?* She leaned against the wall and inhaled deeply, wanting to savor this moment, the culmination of many small, unspoken acts of bravery.

CHAPTER 14

After yet another restless night, Monroe crawled out of bed and dragged herself to the bathroom. She stood in front of the mirror, examining the ever-darker circles under her eyes. Her arms felt heavy and her movements were lethargic, but she reached for her toothbrush anyway. Robotically brushing her teeth and washing her face, her only thought was how desperately she longed to sleep. Too exhausted to read, she left her book on her nightstand and headed down for breakfast. She stopped in front of her Warhol, captivated by Marilyn's expression. *Hmm. Today is August fifth, Tash's birthday. Isn't that the day they found your body, Marilyn? How your death must have shattered the myth people cling to, that a perfect life exists. But it wasn't about them, it was about you. I do wonder what happened. Perhaps you were you just so tired, tired of all of it, that you decided to sleep forever. Maybe it was subconscious. We'll never know, and yet, I feel I understand somehow.* She stood for a moment, blankly staring at the painting. *I should wish Tash a happy birthday.*

***

After spending the day watching her favorite films, a birthday tradition, Tash treated herself to Chinese takeout in bed. She maneuvered some lo mein out of the box, tipped her head back, and sucked down the noodles. There was something comforting about the feel of chopsticks between her fingers and a takeout container on her lap. It reminded her of late nights in New York watching TV in bed with Jason and Penelope. She smiled, grateful that her life was no longer about forgetting but remembering. Before long, she had finished the last spring roll and it was time to get ready for her party.

Thinking it would be a downer to dress up like Jem when Aidan wasn't there to be Rio, she had decided to go as Susan, the title character from *Desperately Seeking Susan*. She put her favorite playlist on shuffle, laughing when Foreigner's "Urgent" came on. Opting to go big or go home, she gave her makeup an eighties vibe with heavily shadowed eyes, rosy cheeks, and rouge-stained lips. She styled her hair in large ringlets at the ends, admiring herself before getting dressed. Decked out in black pants, a black bustier, sparkle boots, and several strands of rhinestones and faux pearls, she looked like she stepped right out of the film. As she admired herself in the full-length mirror, her phone beeped. The driver Aidan hired was waiting outside. *Time to get into the groove*, she thought, winking at herself before grabbing her purse and heading out the door.

***

Tash arrived at the club to see a line around the corner and many people dressed up in eighties attire. There were two signs outside that said, "Come Party '80s Style," and a third directing birthday party guests to the VIP entrance. Tash headed to the VIP door where she was given a wristband for drinks. "Happy Birthday! Have a blast," the bouncer said. She smiled and walked inside. Immediately, her group of friends and the club regulars cheered. Tash blushed. The entire place was decorated with neon twinkly lights and streamers. The bar was running a special on "Tash's Tequila Sunrise," and a half-naked male model was passing out feather boas. Tash smiled hard. *Oh, Aidan. I can't believe you remembered that night in New York.*

As she made her way through the crowd, friends wished her a happy birthday, and soon, strangers did too. Texas was among the well-wishers. He tipped his head and said, "Happy Birthday!" She tipped her head in return, put her hands on her heart, and said, "Thank you. Really, thank you." He smiled and walked off. Tash continued to the bar, where she was promptly handed a cocktail. As she was chatting with the bartender, someone tapped her shoulder. She put her drink down and turned around to see Jason. Her eyes lit up, her jaw dropped, and she started screaming, "Oh my God! I can't believe you're here! I can't believe you flew in from New York! Oh my God!"

Jason laughed and pulled her to him. They hugged each other tightly for so long it was as if time stopped. When they finally released, Tash had tears in her eyes.

"I could fucking kill you," she said, smacking his chest. "My makeup is gonna be a mess."

He laughed. "That's the price you pay for my presence. But get your shit together, we don't want to make a scene."

"I can't believe you're here. I'm so happy!" As Tash sniffled, trying to pull herself together, she got a better look at Jason. He was wearing a shiny purple blazer and had matching purple spray layered over his black hair. "What's with the purple?"

"Aidan said you were coming as Jem. I'm your Rio. But I see you're doing the Madonna thing instead," he said, taking her hand and twirling her around. "I dig it."

"Aidan told you?" she asked, searching her purse for a tissue.

"He called me as soon as he found out he had to miss your party. He bought me a plane ticket and put me up in a hotel so I could surprise you."

"I can't believe he did that," Tash said, dabbing her eyes, careful not to smudge her makeup.

"Yes, you can."

Tash looked down, smiling. "Yeah, he's the best."

"So, I need a drink and then we dance."

Tash nodded. She wiped her nose, stuffed the tissue in her pocket, and got Jason's drink. They clinked glasses.

"To you being more fabulous than ever!" Jason said.

"And to you being here," Tash added.

"Cheers and Happy Birthday, T," Jason said.

"Cheers."

A-ha's "Take on Me" came on and everyone in the club cheered. Tash patted Jason's chest. "Oh my God. I love this song so much. Too perfect."

"Yeah. Aidan really outdid himself," Jason said, scanning the room.

"Speak of the devil," Tash said, retrieving her vibrating phone from her pocket. "He's calling."

"Hey there," she said loudly over the music, pressing her fingers to her free ear to block out the sound.

"Did my present arrive?"

"He's here. I can't believe you did this. I was so surprised."

"That was the plan, beauty queen."

"It's the best present I ever got."

"Aw, shucks," Aidan said, with a laugh. "So, tell me, how are you?"

Tash inhaled deeply. "Slowly learning that life is okay."

Aidan laughed. "That's my girl. Get back to your party. Tell Jason he's the man."

"Yeah, I will." She paused before saying, "And Aidan, thank you."

After Tash hung up, Jason took her hand and led her to the dance floor. They danced for twenty minutes before taking a break to get some water. Engrossed in conversation, they were startled when Lu and Paisley joined them. Lu was dressed in black leather pants and a white T-shirt. She claimed to be an eighties singer but Tash heckled her for looking practically the same as she always does. In contrast, Paisley went all out. She was dressed as Rainbow Brite, complete with rainbows painted on her cheeks, arms, and legs. Jason took one look at her and said, "See, Tash? I told you Rainbow Brite was gay!" They all laughed.

They spent hours drinking, dancing, and laughing. At one point, someone put a white feather boa around Tash's shoulders. She stood in the middle of the dance floor, surrounded by her friends and hundreds of bodies in motion, feathers flying in the air and lightness in her heart.

***

Monroe slipped on her favorite gray silk nightgown and matching robe, and tied the sash around her waist. She opened her nightstand drawer and retrieved the unopened prescription bottle. Sitting on the edge of her bed and rolling the bottle in her hand, it occurred to her that she felt no emotion whatsoever. No sadness, or despair, or grief held her hand. Exhaustion was her only companion. She was done. After moving the bottle from one hand to the other, over and over again, she tucked it into her pocket. She got up and wandered through her house until she found Bill in his office, hunched over the desk.

"It's so late, darling. Why don't you come to bed?" she asked.

"I'll be there soon enough. I have to get through these papers first," he said, gesturing to the stack on his desk.

"Goodnight, Bill. I love you. Truly, I do," Monroe said, before gently shutting the door behind her.

She bumped into Henry on her way back to her bedroom.

"Goodnight, Henry," she said softly.

"Goodnight, Mrs. Preston. Oh, I forgot to tell you that Miss Daniels left her short film here yesterday. She said you had asked to see it."

"Oh, that's right. I did promise her," she mumbled to herself. Then she refocused on Henry. "Maybe I'll watch it now. I know it's late, but would you mind putting it on for me in the screening room?"

"Certainly, ma'am," Henry replied.

Monroe settled into one of the raspberry-colored velvet seats in their lavish private screening room. Henry switched the lights off as the film began. Light from the screen flickered on Monroe's face as the opening credits rolled. Shot in black and white, the camera zoomed in on two young people on a city rooftop in the middle of the night. They were laughing and running across the roof, bits of paper swept up in the breeze. A burst of hot pink leapt off the screen, followed by eruptions of turquoise and purple. Monroe leaned closer. The corners of her mouth trembled and a smile began to crawl across her face. She leaned closer and let the glow from the screen wash over her. Her smile morphed into laughter and tears flooded her eyes. As her smile grew and her laughter became louder, the tears flowed harder. Her face was drenched by the time the closing credits rolled. She sat, soaking in a feeling she couldn't quite name, a feeling she knew was connected to life itself.

Henry returned and flipped the lights on. "Shall I close the room for you before I retire to bed?" he asked.

She wiped her face with her palms and turned to face him. "No. Henry, please get Bill right away. Tell him there's something he must see."

PART THREE

CHAPTER 15

Lu woke up to find Paisley's arm slung across her chest. Careful not to wake her, she gently maneuvered herself out of bed. As she searched the floor for a T-shirt to slip on, she noticed rainbow paint smeared across her chest and legs. Her hands were sticky, so she looked and discovered more paint. *I told her not to do the face paint*, she thought, although she couldn't help but laugh. *Definitely need strong coffee today*.

Still groggy, she shuffled to the kitchen. Given the demands of her day and night jobs, paired with an unpredictable sleep schedule, it was the smell of coffee that helped denote the start of a new day, whether at seven in the morning or two in the afternoon. So, she ignored the paint on her hands in favor of starting the coffee pot. After hitting the brew button, she went to the bathroom and got a look at herself in the mirror. Her hair was matted on one side and there was a multi-colored streak – red, orange, yellow, green, and blue – on her face. "Well, that's a new look," she mumbled.

She flipped the shower on, praying it would be hot by the time she finished brushing her teeth. She swished mouthwash around until her teeth gleamed. Stepping into the shower, she breathed a deep sigh of relief. The water was hot. She rubbed the bar of soap in her hands until it lathered, and then she scrubbed the rainbow splotches in a circular motion. The colors started to meld together, creating a light film of color all over her body. It dawned on her that she was quite literally covered in Paisley. Suddenly, the paint felt like more than an amusing annoyance. It was getting harder to tell where she ended and Paisley began. This made her uncomfortable. She didn't want to think about it, so as she had done for most of her life, she focused on the task at hand and pushed the distressing thoughts to the far edge of her mind. She took the bar of soap and vigorously rubbed it directly on her body, watching the colors trickle down until they circled the drain. When the water ran clear, she could breathe again.

Lu emerged from the bathroom, drying her hair with a towel. Paisley called from the kitchen, startling her.

"I just poured myself a cup of coffee. You want some?"

"Fuck," Lu grumbled, having just pulled a muscle in her neck.

"You okay?" Paisley called.

"Yeah, just a neck strain. It's fine."

"Coffee?" Paisley asked again.

"Yeah, please," Lu replied, tossing her towel in the corner. "I thought you'd still be asleep. Did I wake you?" she asked, before taking a seat at the small table.

"The smell did. You know there's paint on the handle of the coffee pot?" Paisley took the milk out of the refrigerator to splash some in Lu's mug.

"Yeah, it pretty much got everywhere."

Paisley bit her lip. She handed Lu a mug of steaming coffee, taking the seat opposite her. "Uh, yeah. Sorry about that. Guess I kinda went overboard."

Lu smiled and blew on her coffee before taking a sip. "That's okay. It's sweet you went all out for Tash. Besides, it's a reminder of a fun night. Better than a hangover, eh?"

Paisley giggled. "I hope Tash had a great time. It seemed like she did."

"She definitely did. I think she spent most of the summer dreading her birthday. It's hard to celebrate when you feel low, but she's doing a lot better. I can tell. Having Jason there meant the world to her."

"I guess I was sort of dreading it, too. I mean, not the party, per se, but just that it's a marker of time. I've been thinking about how the summer's almost over." Paisley looked down, as if searching for the words. "I start teaching again soon."

"That's right," Lu said. "I almost forgot."

"Yeah, well, the thing is I won't be able to be on your schedule anymore. I mean, I'll be working during the day, so I won't be able to go to clubs as much and you know always crash here."

Lu silently sipped her coffee and Paisley continued.

"I mean, I can come on the weekends, but…"

"Look, I get it. This summer has been amazing, but you need to get back to your life."

"Well, I wouldn't exactly put it that way. You're obviously a part of my life. A big part. But things will change." She looked at her feet, something obviously on her mind.

Lu slipped her hand into Paisley's hand and asked, "What is it?"

"Come to my place tomorrow. My folks invited us over for brunch. They've been dying to meet you."

Lu pulled her hand away and shifted back in her seat. "I'm not so great with parents. Never been into the whole family thing."

"They're not like that. You'll like each other; they're cool. My mom's really into music. And they're important to me, so I want you to know each other. Besides, if you met them, maybe you'd be more comfortable staying at my place sometimes. I'm sure you've avoided it because of the whole parents thing. You'll see that the guest house is actually really private. That way, when I'm teaching, we could maybe go back and forth."

Lu inhaled and took another sip of coffee.

"It's just brunch. I promise, you'll like them."

Lu looked down, squirming in her seat, and then looked up at Paisley. She noticed the flecks of aquamarine sparkling in her eyes, the brown freckle on the tip of her nose, and the soft pink indent at the edge of her upper lip: the beautiful rainbow of Paisley's face of which she never tired. "Yeah, okay. I'll come to brunch. I have to open the juice bar, but I can take off at eleven."

Paisley crinkled her face into a silly smile as her cheeks reddened. She put her mug down and leaned forward to kiss Lu. Then she jumped up and said, "I'm taking a shower."

Lu continued drinking her coffee, wondering what she had gotten herself into. Paisley was thinking about the future, and what's more, how their futures were tied together. Lu was fiercely independent, "an island," Tash always joked. She had never allowed herself to need another or to be needed. The idea of a family being more than a random group with whom meals and homes are forcibly and temporarily shared was foreign to her. She had no interest in spending time with family, including her own, whom she visited once a year on Thanksgiving out of obligation and spoke to on the phone only a few times more. Although she periodically flirted with feelings of guilt for her lack of interest in people she described as "good folks who did their best," those thoughts were few and far between. She rarely thought of them at all.

As she listened to the water from the shower, Lu wondered what she would tell Paisley's parents about herself. She hated answering questions about her upbringing. Her peers simply accepted her as Lu K, hot LA deejay, but older people always asked her "real" name. She never understood why people were so interested in something she felt had nothing to do with who she was. What a boring question.

Lucille Kowalski grew up in Cincinnati in a nuclear family hovering on the edge of the middle class. They were impossibly ordinary: her father, a sales clerk; her mother, a nurse; her older brother, a high school hockey player; and Lu, a misfit. To Lu, it seemed they were all dwelling in the same space without rhyme or reason, random cohabitants. The only real time they spent together, aside from holidays and annual back-to-school shopping, was at the dinner table. Lu's mother insisted they eat together every night, at six o'clock on the dot. Lu sat at the rectangular, Formica table each night to eat a dinner that didn't taste quite right and make small talk that didn't sound quite right.

For as long as she could remember, she had a passion for music, although for years there was little she could do about it. Her school offered music classes, but they were full of uninterested kids clanging away on bongos and tambourines. When she was twelve, her grandparents gave her a small, preprogrammed keyboard designed for kids. She played with it every day, finding ways to push it beyond its bounds. At the age of thirteen, her parents indulged her with weekly piano lessons, but without the ability to practice at home she never got far, and they eventually decided it wasn't worth the money. When she began high school, she realized how limited her exposure to music had been, mostly rock, pop, and classical. At fourteen, she discovered other kinds of music: electronica, trap, hip-hop, trip-hop, and techno. She loved anything with an interesting beat. She became fascinated with creating and digitally altering music. When she attended her first high school party, some kid's older brother was deejaying. He wasn't merely playing existing music, but rather, creating his own mixes.

A new world opened to her. She wanted to learn everything she could about music production and deejaying. She begged her parents for a laptop, deejay turntables, a mixer, and other basic equipment, but they said it was too extravagant. They always paid for her brother's sports equipment. It felt terribly unfair. Was it because she was a girl? Was it because her interest was somehow less valid? Did they not take her seriously? These questions haunted her. She concluded that a girl with a dream is on her own in the world. She spent the next year mowing lawns and babysitting, even though she was ill-suited for the latter. By the time she was fifteen, she had hobbled together the equipment she needed, all second-hand, and began the long road of self-education.

Lu studied her family during the long silences at dinner. She was taller than her mother, lankier than her father and brother, and looked as out of place as she felt. One night, as she swirled the tuna casserole around her plate, it dawned on her: *I must be adopted.* The thought brought instant relief. Suddenly, she had an explanation; she didn't feel like one of them because she wasn't. The next time she was home alone, she searched the cobweb-filled attic for some proof of her lineage: a baby blanket with another name, a stack of unopened mail from her birth mother, or her real birth certificate. When she didn't find anything, she crept into her parent's room and rifled through their drawers. The only noteworthy things she discovered were a secret stash of Oreo cookies her father was hiding and a stack of poems tucked away in her mother's underwear drawer. The poems were in her mother's handwriting, although she had never known her to have the slightest interest in the arts. That was the first and only time she ever thought her mother's life may not have been as boring as it seemed.

After coming up empty on her search, the question of her origin festered. One night at dinner, after her father told her brother to rake the leaves that weekend, to which her brother merely grunted in response, Lu couldn't hold it in anymore. She looked around the table and blurted out, "So, am I adopted or something?"

Her mother casually replied, "What a strange thing to say."

"That's not an answer," Lu said, more convinced than ever.

Her brother laughed. "I wish you were adopted so we could send you back."

Lu ignored him and pressed her mother. "So, am I? It's okay, I just want to know."

"No, you're not adopted. Why on earth would you say that?" her mother replied.

"Because it's the only thing that would explain it, explain us. Haven't you noticed that we don't have anything in common? Not a single thing!"

"I don't understand. We're a family. Is this about that band you want to see?" her mother asked.

Her father sighed. "Not that again. It's past your curfew and that part of town isn't safe."

Lu shook her head. "I told you, it's not a band. It's an open mic night. I want to perform. If I'm gonna do something in art or music, I need experience."

"Maybe you could be an elementary school music teacher," her mother said.

"If she's going to be a teacher, she should teach math or history. That's more stable," her father added.

Lu sat in disbelief before shouting, "What are you talking about? I don't want to be a teacher!"

"Well, you don't need to decide now," her mother said.

Lu opened her mouth, but knew there was no adequate response. These people had no idea who she was and they never would. She looked around the table and silently screamed: *How the fuck can I be one of you?*

The next day, Lu stopped at the cheap hair salon in their local shopping center and got her hair cut very short, "edgy," as she instructed the stylist. That night at dinner, her brother said, "You look like a boy." She replied, "And you look like an idiot." Her parents never said a word, as if they hadn't noticed the loss of ten inches. Lu knew they were too uncomfortable to acknowledge it and so they ignored it. While she had never uttered the words out loud, Lu considered that to be the day she boldly and unapologetically came out, both about her sexuality and musical career path. From that moment on, she considered herself a free agent, free from the pretense of caring about other people's expectations.

Two weeks later, she snuck out to go to the open mic night. She paid her brother twenty dollars to cover for her. When it was her turn on stage, she recited a spoken-word poem she had written for the occasion, set to music. The poem needed work, but her delivery and sense of musicality were compelling. Even at the age of fifteen, she possessed the charisma to command attention. She was invited to come back. And so began her years of performing in coffee shops, bookstores, bars, and anywhere else that would give her a stage. She met older artists and musicians, some of whom were catty, which taught her to always watch her back. Others became friends "from the scene," although sensing there was somewhere bigger and better in her future, she tried not to get too attached. She frequently found herself in sticky situations. Some nights, drunk men heckled her, other nights they hit on her. These encounters forced her to learn how to negotiate personal safety. One night, a man followed her to the bus stop, making lewd comments. She eventually whirled around and said, "Look buddy, it's not happening. I like girls." He got right in her face and started screaming homophobic slurs, his spit hitting her cheeks. He threatened to "give it to her good," claiming that "a real man would fix you." She was terrified but did her best to hide it, jumping on the first bus that came by. She thought about asking the bus driver for help, but was unsure if she could trust him either. She concluded she was on her own and could no longer risk certainty about people. From that night on, Lu wore her distrust like armor, even when it was exhausting and lonely to do so. She learned to carry herself with attitude and confidence at all times. At the urging of a twenty-something gay man she befriended at a slam poetry event, she began seeking out LGBTQA-friendly venues. She felt an uncomfortable mixture of gratitude for these safer spaces and resentment at the need for them. They made her world at once bigger and smaller. Over time, she developed her persona as Lu K and built a small and loyal following.

When she was seventeen, her brother left for college and her mother began working the night shift. So ended family dinners. This worked well for Lu, who was busy living her authentic life, one her parents didn't care to know about. After a string of casual encounters with girls from school, she met Jenna at a club when she was eighteen.

Lu cared for her but could never truly match Jenna's feelings, but when Jenna prepared to move across the country, Lu jumped at the chance to go with her. She left Cincinnati determined to find her people, even though she was equally determined not to need them.

This all came rushing back as she drank her coffee and thought about meeting Paisley's parents, and then as she thought about Paisley, her softness and goodness. Eventually, she heard the shower turn off. *Fuck, I need to get out of my head. Coffee, I need more coffee.* She slurped the last bit in her mug and got up for a refill, stretching her neck, still strained from earlier when Paisley startled her. *Damn*, she thought. She searched the cabinets for Advil, but the bottle was empty so she settled for another cup of coffee. When she put the pot down, she noticed her hand was sticky again. She looked to see a rainbow splotch in the middle of her palm.

CHAPTER 16

Monroe's eyelashes were stuck together, with thick layers of crust in the corners. She wiped away the crust and slowly opened her eyes. She couldn't remember the last time she felt so rested. It was as if she had slept for days. She turned to look at the clock on her nightstand. It was almost noon. She stretched her arms, reached for her silk robe, and sauntered into the bathroom. When she saw her reflection in the mirror, she thought, *I know you*. Then she glanced at the small picture of her mother. She picked it up and whispered, "I think I know you too, Mama. Rest well." As she moved to put the photo down, she heard a slight rustling noise and realized she still had the pill bottle in the pocket of her robe. She retrieved the bottle and confidently tossed it in the trash. After freshening up, she grabbed the book on her nightstand and headed to the breakfast room. On her way, she bumped into Henry.

"Good morning, Mrs. Preston, or perhaps I should say good afternoon."

"I can't believe how well I slept, Henry. I feel marvelous."

"Shall I have the cook prepare your usual breakfast or would you prefer lunch?"

"Perhaps an egg white omelet and we'll call it brunch."

"Very good, Mrs. Preston. Shall I bring your book?"

"Thank you, Henry," she said, handing him the book.

Henry hurried off to inform the cook. Monroe strolled through her home, absentmindedly humming. This time, when she stopped by her Warhol, she saw it with fresh eyes.

Oh Marilyn, thank you for helping me to see. I finally understand what you meant, about life slipping further away. Some of us use glamour as armor, or perhaps as a mask. Others of us prefer to dwell in isolation. No matter the path, we can never hide from ourselves. We can't stop the feelings in all shades of light and dark. She stood for a moment and then smiled, mischievously. *I'm glad Mr. Warhol captured this part of you, the smile just a bit too bright. He was clever. Rest well, dear Marilyn.* Monroe walked away knowing she had finally made peace with something that could not be named and knowing that the painting that had once captivated her would now take on a welcome ordinary quality.

She practically floated into the breakfast room. She poured herself a cup of coffee and picked up her book, left on the table for her. Before she could open it, the cook walked in and presented her meal.

"This looks delicious. Thank you," Monroe said.

"May I get you anything else?"

"My cell phone, please. I must have left it upstairs." *I need to get in touch with Tash right away.*

***

"Oooh, this is so Cali," Jason said, as he took his seat on the patio at Café Gratitude.

"Yeah, it's kind of hot today but I knew you'd want to sit outside. It's *the* it spot. I once saw Jennifer Lopez here."

"How'd she look?"

"Flawless, of course. She was wearing a short, gold, tunic-style dress, and I would have killed to know what brand of highlighter she was using. Her cheekbones, like *wow*."

"Forget the celebs. Look at the waiters. My oh my," Jason said, lifting his dark sunglasses to get a better look.

"You're such a slut," Tash joked.

"Uh huh," Jason said.

"I can't believe you're moving in with your boyfriend. That's so grown-up. But I can see you haven't lost your wandering eye," Tash said, as Jason strained his neck to look at the waiter.

"Looking is good. Keeps us healthy. It's like yoga for the libido."

Tash laughed. "I do have to admit the waiters here are seriously hot and they have this chill, Zen thing going on that makes 'em even hotter."

"Speaking of," Jason said softly as their waiter approached.

"My name is Brock and I'll be taking care of you today. Welcome to Café Gratitude. Have you dined with us before?" he asked as he filled their water glasses.

"I have," Tash said.

"It's my first time," Jason said coyly.

Tash rolled her eyes.

"Welcome. Would you like to hear today's question?"

"Absolutely," Jason said.

"Today's question is: In what ways are you growing? I'll give you a few minutes with the menu and check back."

As he walked away, Tash shook her head. "You are positively shameless."

"Brock. His name is Brock. I mean, *hello*. God, I love LA."

Tash giggled. "I missed you so much."

"Me too."

"We're not really answering that lame question, are we?"

"Hell no. I just wanted the pretty man to stay at the table longer. Okay, so what's good here?" Jason asked, picking up his menu.

"It's totally vegan, but the food is amazing. They have great pressed juices and smoothies you'd love. They do breakfast 'til one on the weekends and I know how you love brunch."

"Oh my God, I love the names of things."

"Yeah, when you order something, they'll compliment you based on the name they've given the food you order. Like if I order a muffin, he'll call me beautiful. It's so LA."

"Do you ever order based on what you want the hot waiter to say to you? I totally would," Jason mused.

Tash laughed. "I'm not as hard up for compliments as you are."

"Yes, you are."

Tash crinkled her face.

"The doughnut is called holy. That's adorbs," Jason said. "Isn't there some nineties song that goes something like 'you'll never gain weight from a doughnut hole?' Kind of heavy for brunch, huh?"

Tash shrugged.

Soon, Brock returned to take their order. "What can I get you, Miss?"

"I'll have an Arabica coffee and the superfood granola, please."

"You are courageous and powerful," Brock said.

Jason smirked.

"And for you?"

"I'll have the energy juice and the buckwheat flax pancakes, please."

"Would you like to add berries or cashew whipped cream?"

"Let's live a little. I'll add it all," Jason replied.

"You are succulent and open-hearted," Brock said.

Jason smiled. "Indeed I am."

Brock grabbed their menus and walked away. Tash shook her head. "You are so bad. And since when do you eat carbs?"

"I'm treating myself. I mean, cashew whipped cream. How could I pass that up? Damn, I love LA. I can't believe you don't."

"I never said that."

Jason took his sunglasses off and placed them on the table. "Oh, please. It's me."

Tash looked down.

"Tell me."

"I don't want to be a downer," she replied.

"Sweetie, I didn't come all this way for fake talk."

"It's been a really big adjustment. In the beginning it was great, but then..." she trailed off as Brock returned with their drinks.

Jason took a sip of his green juice. "Come on, how could you not love this?" he asked, holding up the glass.

"Gross. It looks like sludge."

Jason laughed, but then his expression turned more serious. "What happened? Was it the dead ends with your film? If they don't get it, screw them. You're ahead of your time."

"Not being able to make anything happen was depressing, but then... God, I feel like a piece of shit for even thinking it..."

"When Aidan got a break, it was hard as hell and you wanted to pull your hair out. Metaphorically, of course. Your hair is fab."

"You know how much I love him and how talented he is. I mean, if anyone deserves..."

Jason interrupted. "You don't have to do that with me. I get it. Aidan's awesome. We all love him. Not the point. You can want good things for him and still feel that it's not fair."

"Thanks. I guess I really needed to say it out loud to release it."

"What about Lu? Can't you talk to her about this?"

Tash raised her eyebrows. "Are you kidding me? She's been working the LA club scene way longer than Aidan. It's tough for her too. Tougher than she'd admit."

Jason took another sip of his juice. "How's the summer gone while he's been away?"

"Honestly, I wasted most of it. I just couldn't try anymore. I couldn't keep putting myself out there just to be rejected. But then I decided, *fuck it*. Regardless of what happens, I'm going to make art. That's how I got the show I have next week. I crawled my way back to myself."

"Which is freaking amazing," Jason said. "See? The waiter was right; you *are* courageous and powerful."

Tash blushed.

"I guess we answered that inane question-of-the-day after all. Sounds like you're growing in lots of ways."

"You too, sweetie. I mean, a full-time man and a full-time job. That's a big change! I'm so proud of you for starting your own interior design business. You're gonna crush it. And you never looked better."

Jason smiled. "And Pen! She was always a grown-up, but now that she's getting married, I mean, like wow. And he's so perfect for her. You'll see at the wedding next summer. He's really nerdy and loves talking about dusty old history things. They're adorable together."

Tash smiled. "Just as long as she doesn't make me wear something awful at the wedding."

"Oh, honey, you're fucked for sure. I'm picturing pink taffeta, hopefully with lots of ruffles."

Tash shook her head and laughed. "You're such a shit. I can't believe you have to head back tomorrow."

"I know, the price of having an actual job. Modeling was so much better."

"Well, on the plus side, you never would have ordered pancakes when you were modeling, and I'm totally taking a bite."

Just then, Brock delivered their food.

"This looks great," Jason said.

"You go ahead. I'm gonna check my phone quickly, to see if Aidan's tried to reach me."

Tash had received a text from Monroe.

```
Hi Tash. I'd like to invite you to the
studio's anniversary party. Please
buy yourself a fabulous gown and put
it on my account. It's only a few days
away, so tell them any alterations
need to be done immediately. Use my
name. I'm sorry for the last-minute
notice. I do hope you can come.
```

Tash was stunned. Monroe had never invited her to an event before. She slipped her phone back in her purse and looked at Jason.

"What?" he asked, with a mouth full of pancakes.

"Uh, so how do you feel about spending the afternoon helping me pick out a designer gown?"

CHAPTER 17

Lu pulled up to Paisley's parent's home, her heart racing from the stress of being nearly twenty minutes late. She cranked the air conditioning in her car, afraid she'd sweat through her shirt and have pit stains when she met Paisley's parents. The sight of the modern, oceanfront mansion did nothing to calm her nerves. As she sat in her car, berating herself for wearing a button-down shirt and trying to catch her breath, the front door to the house opened. Paisley flitted over, her white sundress blowing in the breeze. Lu jumped out of the car.

"I'm so sorry. The line was out the door today and my replacement was late. I changed as quickly as I could and motored, but the traffic was epic."

Paisley smiled. "Don't worry about it. You're not that late. And you look great, but you didn't need to dress up."

"Is it too much?" Lu asked nervously, as she made sure her shirt was tucked in.

Paisley giggled. "You're perfect. My folks are out back. Let's cut through the house to join them and then I can take you around to my place after we eat."

Lu nodded and followed her. They walked into an enormous entryway that opened to an even more enormous living space. Everything was white and airy. The far wall was made entirely of glass, offering an expansive view of the cobalt sea from the moment you entered the house. Even after years in LA, Lu believed that places like this only existed in movies.

"Holy shit," she muttered.

Paisley giggled. "The view is pretty rad, huh?"

"Uh, yeah. You could say that."

"Come on," Paisley said, taking her hand.

They walked to the other side of the room and stepped through the sliding glass door onto the patio. The back of the property boasted a long infinity pool overlooking the Pacific. There was a row of lounge chairs facing the pool, a firepit and bar to the left, and a large table to the right, where Paisley's parents were seated under umbrellas. They casually stood up as Lu and Paisley approached.

"Mom and Dad, this is Lu."

Lu stuck her hand out. "So nice to meet you, Mrs...."

Paisley's mother interrupted. "Please, call me Ivy."

"And I'm Paul," Paisley's father said, outstretching his hand.

Lu smiled. "I'm so sorry I'm late. I had trouble getting out of work and then the traffic was terrible."

"Don't worry about it. We're enjoying the beautiful day," Ivy said. Lu noticed how much Paisley resembled her. Ivy was taller and thinner, but they had the same coloring: hair, eyes, and complexion.

Paul was a slight man with light brown hair and glasses. "The traffic gets worse each year," he said, sitting down.

"Shall we?" Ivy said, indicating they should all take a seat. "You know, sometimes I think that when Paul retires, we should pack up and move to the mountains to get away from all the congestion here. Maybe Montana. It's beautiful there."

"She says that, but she could never leave the ocean," Paul said with a smile.

"He's probably right," Ivy conceded. "I've been spoiled. There's nothing like doing yoga on the beach. I don't know if I could give it up."

Lu smiled. "Your home is spectacular."

Just then, a staff member came over with carafes of freshly squeezed orange and grapefruit juice.

"Theresa, this is Lu," Paisley said.

"Nice to meet you," Lu said.

"Can I get you coffee or tea?"

"Coffee would be great, thank you."

"For me too, please, Theresa. Oh, and Lu takes milk," Paisley said.

Lu glanced at Paisley, thinking that no one had ever really known her well enough to remember her likes or dislikes before.

Ivy turned to Lu and said, "Please help yourself to some juice, if you'd like."

"I got it," Paisley said, picking up the pitcher of orange juice and pouring some for Lu and then for herself.

"Thanks," Lu said, taking a sip. "Wow, that's delicious. Sweeter than what we've had in the store lately."

"Paisley told us you have a part-time job at a juice bar," Ivy said. "I'm a big juicer. I do a detox at least once a month."

Lu smiled. "Yeah, I've been there for years. I'm the assistant manager. But honestly, it's just a way to pay the bills."

Ivy grinned. "Yes, we've heard you're a gifted deejay. I think it's admirable to do whatever it takes to live as an artist. I could tell you stories about famous musicians I've worked with who walked dogs, washed cars, and bussed tables to make ends meet. That's how you know the real artists: their willingness to work hard because they have to find a way for their art. It's just in their soul. It's a beautiful thing to be around that energy. That's what drew me to the music business."

"You'd be surprised, but it's the same in the tech world, at least for the real creatives who tinker in their parents' garages because they've got some wonderfully bonkers idea they can't let go of no matter how many times they fail. Some people breathe invention and they've just got to spend their lives discovering and creating," Paul said.

Lu smiled, nodding along. It hadn't been five minutes and she already felt that these people saw her, understood her, and what's more, they embraced what mattered most to her. She felt more at home with them than she ever did with her parents. She liked them.

Theresa and another staff member returned with coffee and brunch: an eggless vegetable frittata, fruit salad, and a mesclun salad with tahini dressing.

Once everyone was served, Lu said, "This looks great."

"Most of it came from my mom's vegetable garden, even the herbs."

Paul chuckled. "Be glad it doesn't come from Paisley. This one couldn't keep a cactus alive. She could kill weeds."

"Dad," Paisley whined.

"It's true," Paul insisted, taking a bite of salad.

Paisley turned deep crimson.

"You've always been wonderful with animals, but your dad's right. You didn't inherit my green thumb," Ivy added.

Paisley rolled her eyes. "At least I'm good with bunnies."

Ivy laughed. "You'll always have bunnies."

Lu loved the playful banter. It was clear they were all connected in a special way.

"So, tell me more about your music, Lu," Ivy said. "When did you begin developing your sound?"

They spent the next hour eating, talking about music, and gently teasing Paisley. Ivy was a fount of knowledge about music, and Lu loved listening to her stories about the industry. She thought she'd never stop laughing when Ivy told her about a party at which two members of the Rolling Stones were almost thrown out because someone thought they were homeless people who wandered in off the street. Ivy also knew what the industry was like for women. She said, "It's always tougher for women. If there's ever anything I can do for you," but Lu quickly declined and moved the conversation forward. Paul was equally disarming, just as Paisley had described. In meeting them, she understood Paisley better. They all made sense together. As comfortable as Lu felt with them, there remained a small, nagging discomfort. She fit easily into their dynamic. Things never came easily. She didn't know how to trust it.

***

"You can see it's a lot cozier than the main house" Paisley said, waving her arms around.

"It's great," Lu said. "It's kind of dope to have a two-room house."

"When I was in high school, I begged my folks to let me live here. They wouldn't let me, but my friends and I would sneak in here whenever it wasn't being used. Once I caught one of the guys from Aerosmith in here with a half-naked model. That's a funny story. I was banned from the guesthouse for months. I know I need to move eventually, but it's been great to finally be allowed to live here."

Lu smiled.

"Take a load off on the couch. I'm just gonna grab us some water," Paisley said.

Lu plopped down. She picked up an art book from the coffee table and started flipping through it.

"You should take my mom up on her offer, if there's ever anyone you want to meet or something," Paisley hollered.

"That's really nice of her and all, but there's no way I would ever ask her for a favor."

"She doesn't mind. She loves helping musicians. If you're too shy to ask, I could do it for you."

Lu put the book back on the coffee table. "No way. Please, don't."

Paisley walked over and handed her a glass of water before taking the seat next to her. "Okay, but I don't see what the big deal is."

"Can we just drop it?" Lu asked.

"Yeah, sure," Paisley said. She tilted her head toward the book Lu had been looking at. "Someone gave me that because the Hockney on the cover reminded them of this place. I don't really see it though. To me there's something unbelievable about his work. It's all surface."

"Yeah, I was never a huge fan, but I can see the resemblance. I mean, this place has a sort of hyper-real, picture-perfect quality."

Paisley giggled. "Yeah, it's kind of a postcard. But what's inside is real. So now that you've seen it and met my folks, can you picture yourself spending some time here?"

Lu squirmed. "The thing is, Malibu is way too far from work for me."

"Yeah, and your place is far from my work."

"Yeah, it's a drag. You know the crazy hours I work. I can't be on the road all the time."

Paisley huffed and shook her head. "I'm not suggesting we always stay here."

"I just don't see how I could ever really come this far."

"Of course you don't. That would mean you'd have to consider someone other than yourself."

"Excuse me?" Lu bellowed, leaping up.

Paisley took a deep breath, steadied her nerves, and then looked up at Lu. "You don't care if it works between us. You can take it or leave it."

"That's not fair," Lu said. "I'm here now."

"When I told you that school is starting soon and things would have to change, you assumed that meant we were over. And you didn't even care. I mean, that was your first thought. You made it pretty clear. And I..."

"What?" Lu asked.

"I can't do it anymore. We don't want the same things. I want to find a way to make it work, to make us work, and you don't even care if we break up. You won't meet me halfway and I can't keep doing it for both of us and hoping or pretending."

"If that's how you feel, maybe I should go."

"Yeah, I guess maybe you should."

Without hesitation, Lu walked out the door. Her heart was racing again, but this time with an overwhelming feeling of regret. Too proud or perhaps too afraid to deal with these uncomfortable feelings, she scurried to her car and headed home.

For the next three days, she focused on each task at hand, whether it was peeling carrots at the juice bar or spinning at the club. Yet no matter how hard she tried to push Paisley out of her mind, she kept slipping in.

CHAPTER 18

Tash finished washing off the green face mask she applied to make her skin luminous. She was patting her face dry when her phone beeped. There was a text message from Lu.

> Hey. You're probably getting ready for that fab Hollywood thing, so no sweat if you don't have time. Just feeling meh. Text if you have a minute.

She immediately dialed Lu's number.

"Hey," Lu said. "You didn't have to call. I know it's a big night for you."

"The driver's not picking me up for two hours. What's going on?"

"Do you think I'm really screwed up?"

"Define *really*," Tash joked.

Lu let out a small laugh. "It's like I'm standing at a precipice and I want to take the leap, I really do, but I'm afraid of…"

"Of smashing to the ground and shattering into a million pieces?"

"Thanks for the vivid image!" Lu joked. "But seriously, what if I crash?"

"Yeah, that could happen. But what if you fly?"

Lu sighed.

"Listen, I get it. I do. You've gotta do what feels right for you. I just know from experience that being the invincible cool girl takes a toll. It's a lot easier when we have people who get us so we can let our guard down from time to time."

"It's gonna sound stupid, but I never thought I'd need someone, you know?"

"Needing someone isn't half as scary as being needed. Maybe that's what you're really afraid of. But it makes you rise. And push yourself. It's easy to get lazy in ways we don't even recognize."

Lu exhaled. "It probably doesn't matter anyway. I fucked it up."

"Oh please," Tash said. "You can fix it. You've just gotta decide what you really want."

"I want Paisley."

"Then why are you wasting time with me?"

"Promise me one thing," Lu said. "If it doesn't work out, we never had this conversation."

Tash giggled. "You know it. Good luck."

"Thanks. And have an amazing time tonight. You're probably gonna meet so many of your heroes."

"Totally. You should see the guest list. I still can't believe Monroe invited me. I wish Aidan was here to go with me."

"He'll be back soon, right?" Lu asked.

"Yeah, and I'll be busy 'til then anyway. I have work to do for Monroe, then Tuesday I have to go do the set-up at the gallery. He gets back Wednesday. Then the opening is Thursday night. You'll be there, right?"

"Wouldn't miss it."

"I better go get glamorous. Oh my God, you should see my gown. It looks like liquid gold and has this plunging neckline. It's a showstopper, if I do say so myself. I'm wearing my hair down on one side, with waves. Very old-school Hollywood. And of course, bright red lips."

Lu laughed. "You're gonna crush it. Have fun, babe."

"You too, baby."

*****

After exchanging text messages with Paisley, Lu spent an hour pacing around her apartment, waiting for her to arrive. When she heard a gentle knock, she squeezed her eyes shut for a moment and then opened the door.

"Hey, come on in," she said, closing the door behind her. "Thanks for coming here. I would have come to your place if I wasn't working later tonight."

"It's okay," Paisley said, taking a seat on the edge of Lu's bed. "I wanted to apologize to you anyway."

Lu furrowed her brow and sat down next to her. "*You* wanted to apologize?"

"I overreacted. I was going to reach out, but then you didn't try to get in touch with me, and…"

"I'm the one who should apologize," Lu said, taking a deep breath. "You were just calling me out on my shit. And in some ways, you were spot on. But it's not that I don't care or that I don't want to be with you."

Paisley took Lu's hand. "Then what is it?"

"I want to show you something." Lu jumped up and pulled a photograph out of her dresser drawer.

"What's that?" Paisley asked.

Lu plopped back down on the edge of the bed. "It's a picture of my family."

Paisley took the photo and then looked back at Lu.

"They're nothing like your family. I mean, you guys get each other. No one from my family has any clue about who I am. And they don't even try to learn."

"That must have been tough growing up," Paisley said.

"It made me rely on myself. If I wanted something, I had to find a way to make it happen. I could never count on anyone else to do anything for me. Don't get me wrong, they're not bad people. I don't have a horrible sob story." She looked down as if searching for the words. "When we started dating, you asked me why I moved to the West Coast. You asked what I was trying to get away from. See, the thing is, I wasn't really trying to flee *from* something, but rather *to* something."

Paisley smiled.

"And now I don't want to run at all. I just want to be. I've never felt that way before."

Paisley rubbed Lu's hand.

Lu smiled. "I love you and I want to be with you."

"I love you, too," Paisley said.

Lu leaned in, put her hand on Paisley's face, and kissed her. When she pulled back, Paisley said, "So I guess this means you'll be crashing at my place part of the time."

"Actually, what I said about Malibu being too far from work was true." Paisley looked down and bit her lip. Lu continued. "I was thinking, my lease is up soon. I know it's fast, but I was hoping we could get a place together, somewhere in the middle."

Paisley smiled brightly, grabbed Lu, and they fell into the bed.

***

Tash stepped out of the limousine to a frenzy of flashing lightbulbs. Photographers clicked away as she slowly walked the carpet toward Magic Manor. Meryl and Goldie were walking ahead of her, and one of the directors she most admired was following behind her. *This is unbelievable, even if it is just one Cinderella night.*

She walked inside and was immediately handed a glass of champagne. Waiters walked around with trays of caviar blinis, mini salmon *en croute*, and artichoke hearts topped with mushroom duxelles. She was popping a blini into her mouth when a parlor magician started doing an illusion. People gathered around to watch. By the end of the trick, Tash was laughing and chatting with a few other guests, but they all turned to look when Bill and Monroe arrived. Monroe looked stunning in a strapless, black satin gown, her ears and neck dripping with diamonds. Tash caught Monroe's eye and they both tilted their heads in acknowledgement of each other. Monroe held her finger up as if to say, please wait for me. Tash smiled and continued making small talk as Bill and Monroe greeted their guests. Soon, Tash saw Monroe whisper something to Bill. Then she sashayed across the room.

"Tash, you look gorgeous. I'm so glad you could make it."

"I can't thank you enough for the invitation and the gown. This is one of the most exciting nights of my life."

Monroe smiled.

"Oh, and you look beautiful too, Monroe."

"Thank you. I feel wonderful. I had been suffering from terrible insomnia, but I finally started sleeping soundly again." She paused before continuing, "It's the strangest thing and I'm a bit embarrassed to admit it, but it actually started after you told me about Aidan's tour. For some reason, I couldn't get it out of my mind."

Tash crinkled her face. "I guess it stirred something up for you too."

"There was just something about his fast success that took hold of my mind. I don't know if you remember, but we also spoke about why I came to Los Angeles. I hadn't thought about that in years and, well, it's not important why, but that got my head spinning. So yes, in a strange way, your boyfriend's tour was the impetus for some restless nights."

"I'm glad you're feeling better."

Monroe took Tash's hand and looked at her earnestly. "It was your film. I watched your film." She squeezed Tash's hand. "You had never told me what it was about."

Tash smiled. "That was one of my problems with the film festivals and grant proposals. I was terrible at describing it and I think people misunderstood it or wanted it to be something easier to define, something more Hollywood."

Monroe's eyes widened. "When it started with that couple, I thought it was going to be a love story. But that's not really what it is at all."

Tash shook her head. "No, it's not."

Monroe released Tash's hand and then held her hands up as if trying to animate what the film was about. "It's about that thing inside each of us. That thing, that feeling, you know? Possibilities. It's about possibilities."

Tash smiled. "Yes, that's exactly right. I should have had you help me explain it. People didn't get it."

"Well, I did. And Bill did too. I showed it to him and he thought it was brilliant. Hold on, let me get his attention. That's why I invited you; he wants to chat with you."

Tash was dumbfounded as she watched Monroe wave Bill over.

"Well, hello there," he said, extending his hand. "We've seen each other briefly at the house but I don't think we've properly met."

"It's nice to meet you, sir," Tash said, shaking his hand. "Thank you so much for having me."

"Monroe was quite taken with your film. I know you didn't ask her to show it to me; I hope you don't mind that she did. You can't imagine how many people have asked Monroe to show me their headshots, or scripts, or films. She never has before, not once, so I watched your film with deep curiosity. I can see why she was moved. You have a great sensibility. It showed tremendous promise."

Tash blushed and tried to keep her mouth from falling open. "Thank you. I'm extremely honored."

"Let me cut to the chase. A couple of years ago, we acquired several small production companies. One of them specializes in art films, producing pieces for museum theaters, supporting the shorts, and so on. We had the idea to turn it into something, maybe even work with streaming platforms, but the truth is, we haven't done much with it yet. We need to get some talent in there with vision to curate and develop content. Are you available to come in Monday for an interview and to meet the team?"

Tash's jaw dropped. "Uh, I don't even know what to say."

"Say yes."

"Yes, of course. I'll be there."

"Terrific. I'll have my assistant call you to confirm the details. It was wonderful talking with you, but I can see one of my snippiest screenwriters and snarkiest directors huddled together. They're giving me the eye. If I don't go say hello, they'll make my life hell."

Tash laughed. "Of course. Thank you again for the opportunity."

"I'll join you in a minute, darling," Monroe said.

As soon as Bill walked away, Tash's eyes became misty.

"Oh, don't cry dear, you'll ruin your eye makeup."

"Monroe, I don't know how to thank you. I can't believe you did this for me."

"There's no need to thank me. You're talented, truly talented. Tash, you have a passion. I envy that about you. It's something I always longed for."

Tash smiled.

"Just promise you'll meet me for lunch from time to time and you'll tell me if what I'm wearing belongs on the worst-dressed list."

"Of course," Tash said, sniffling.

"I better join Bill before he thinks I defected. Enjoy yourself tonight. There should be quite a lot of magic."

"I will. Monroe, please know how grateful I am. I think you're extraordinary. And I bet you have more passion in you than you realize. It's never too late."

Monroe smiled and sauntered off.

Tash stood, glowing as brightly as her gown, taking in the feeling, the chatter, and the magic.

CHAPTER 19

Tash was standing in the back of the gallery's media room when Patty popped in to check on her.

"How's the system working?" Patty asked.

"It's great," Tash said, turning to face her. "Projecting it on all three walls was a great idea, especially for the opening running scene. You feel like you're moving with them."

"Glad we could make it work. We were prepared for it from a show we did last year, but I always cross my fingers for anything tech."

Tash smiled. "I hear ya."

"I'm dashing out for a lunch meeting. I'll see you Thursday night."

"I'm just gonna run through it a couple more times to make sure there aren't any glitches with the thirty-second delay between showings. Then I'll set up the chairs and head out myself."

"Ellen's up front if you need anything. Make sure to use the white folding chairs. They're stacked in the back room."

"Okay. Thanks, Patty."

As Patty left, the film ended. Tash walked to the center of the dark, empty room, waiting for the film to restart. She was standing still, her mind quiet, when she heard someone step into the doorway and knock on the wall. Thinking Patty forgot something, she turned, just as the film began again. The light hit her face as her images popped up all around her. She gasped. It was Aidan. He was wearing black leather pants, a t-shirt, headphones slung around his shoulders, and the sexiest smile she had ever seen. "Hey there, beauty queen," he said, leaning against the doorframe.

She smiled as the light and images from her film bounced off her face. "Aidan," she said, as if confirming it was really him. "I thought you weren't coming home until tomorrow."

"Yeah, after you called yesterday with your incredible news, I decided to skip the big party. Hitched a ride with one of the crew who had to get back for his kid's birthday."

"How'd you know where to find me?"

"When I got home, I bumped into Darrell. He told me you'd be here."

Tash smiled.

"So, creative development for an artsy production company, a subsidiary of a major studio. I mean, wow. Holy smokes. That's amazing. Congratulations. I'm so proud of you."

"I still can't believe it. I'll be going through submissions and curating content with two other people, who I met and actually really like. I mean, it's not glamorous, but Aidan, can you believe it?"

Aidan smiled, looked her up and down, and then said, "Yeah, I can believe it."

Tash blushed. "I might be able to pitch some of my own work too."

"I'd expect nothing less," he said, walking over. They stood inches apart, staring at each other as the light from the projector hit their faces.

"So, what have you been up to this summer?" Tash asked.

Aidan slipped the headphones off his shoulders and put them on her ears. "This is something new I've been working on." He put his arms around her waist and hit play. Tash listened to his beats as her images swirled around them both.

After a few minutes, she took off the headphones, leaned in, and kissed him.

"God, I missed you," he said.

"Me too. I love you. I'm sorry for how things were before you left. I had to work through some stuff."

"I know. It's all good. So, you said your new job starts November first. Did Monroe ask you for two months or something?"

"No. She's so amazing, she just let me go. I'm already done. I offered to help her find a replacement, but she said she could find someone. I actually think she's going to do it on her own for a bit. She texted me this morning that she's signing up for a class. She can't decide between writing and fashion design. I think she's trying to figure out what's next for her. You know, find her bliss."

"That's cool."

"Yeah. And I'll still see her. She stops by the studio from time to time and made me promise to meet her for lunches."

"So then why aren't you starting the new job right away?"

"I asked for two months. When I start, I want to give it my all and I really want to write my full-length screenplay first, while I have time. I know I should have done it this summer, but I was going through some stuff and…"

"You don't have to explain."

"I know nothing may come of it, but it's just something I need to see through. So, I'm taking two months off to write. With what we're both making now I figured we could swing it. Is that okay?"

"It's perfect, actually."

Tash raised an eyebrow.

"Calvin's two-week UK tour starts the week after next. We bonded, and as a thank you present, he invited us to come along for a vacation, all expenses paid."

Tash grinned.

"When we were in New York, you asked me if I could deejay in LA. Do you remember?"

"I remember."

"Well, can you write in London? I figured we could use the time together. You can write during the day and we can party at night. The clubs are supposed to be the bomb. We could even catch some theater if you need inspiration. So, what do you say, beauty queen? Are you in?"

She watched the images floating around them, and then looked into his eyes. "I'm all in."

AFTERWORD

It's important to talk about the relationship between *Low-Fat Love*, *Blue*, and *Film*. Tash Daniels first appeared as a supporting character in my debut novel, *Low-Fat Love*. She became the protagonist in *Blue*. When I finished *Blue*, I knew I had another story to tell; *Film* is that story.

I felt strongly that *Film* needed to stand on its own, and that informed how I approached the writing. *Film* can be read as a stand-alone novel or as a sequel to *Blue*. While these three books are not a traditional trilogy, I think of them as installation art. Each novel tells a different story about our relationship to popular culture, our relationship to others, and our own sense of self. *Film* is the final piece in the installation.

At their core, I would describe the books this way: *Low-Fat Love* explores the effect of toxic popular culture on women's lives, *Blue* explores how we may positively use the stories in popular culture to illuminate our own stories, and *Film* explores how the popular culture or art we create sustains us. Further, the characters in *Low-Fat Love* show how people may suffer in isolation, the characters in *Blue* show the importance of having people in our lives who get us, and the characters in *Film* show the importance of developing a strong sense of self as individuals if we are to have healthy and affirming relationships with others. While *Film* can be read on its own, a full picture emerges when the three are read together. To honor the interconnections between these works, there are nods to *Low-Fat Love* and *Blue* in this novel, including specific pop culture references that repeat across the books.

See how Tash and Aidan met, in the first chapter of *Blue*, reprinted at the end of this book.

Patricia Leavy

SUGGESTED CLASSROOM OR BOOK CLUB USE

1. *Film* suggests that the art we make and experience helps shape who we are. Explore this topic in relation to any of the main or supporting characters. What about with yourself or your friends?
2. The word "film" comes up with several characters and takes on different meanings in different contexts. What are the ways the word surfaces, and what does it mean?
   a. Why do you think the novel is titled *Film*?
3. The use of a fictional lens allows for the exploration of characters' pasts as well as their "inner worlds" through techniques such as flashbacks and interior dialogue. Select an example from the book that shows how one of these techniques helped to illustrate the identity issues the character was struggling with.
4. The issue of coping with rape culture – sexual harassment, sexual assault, and intimidation – comes up in each of the main characters' stories. How are these issues reflected in your community or college campus? How, if at all, has the #MeToo Movement or Time's Up initiative changed things?
5. To what extent are the challenges faced by the main characters directly tied to their gender identity as women? Explain using examples from the novel.
6. How are the stories of the three main characters similar? How does the writing connect these women's stories?
7. Popular culture and art are referenced throughout the book. Select a few of these references to explore. How does it influence the character? What, if any, symbolism is evoked? What, if any, metaphors to do you see?
   a. Monroe develops a fascination with an Andy Warhol painting of Marilyn Monroe. Explain what she sees in the painting. Look up one of Warhol's Monroes online. What do you see in the piece after having read this novel?

8. Sociologically, *Film* explores the "front stage" and "back stage" of each main character. Find a few examples of scenes in which we can see how the back stage is influencing the front stage, or where there is a disjuncture between how a character presents herself and the behind-the-scenes reality.
9. How do the characters communicate with each other? What do their patterns of interaction reveal about their relationships?
10. Issues related to privilege surface throughout the book, for example, in mentions of homelessness. Explore this topic using examples from the book and what you think about the characters and their perspectives.

CREATIVE WRITING ACTIVITIES

1. Darrell, Texas, Patty Price, and Bill Preston are minor characters in *Film*. Select one of these characters and write his/her story.
2. Monroe's mother's story is told from Monroe's perspective. Rewrite her story from her own perspective.
3. Select one of the characters and fast forward five years. Write a short story based on where you think they are now.
4. Aidan was on tour for most of the novel. Write a short story about his experience on tour.
5. If *Film* was a play instead of a novel, it would likely include monologues by the main characters. Select a character and write her pivotal monologue.
6. Write Tash's full-length screenplay, remembering that the short version is about "possibilities."
7. Write an alternative ending to *Film*.

QUALITATIVE RESEARCH ACTIVITIES

1. Select several scenes and perform discourse or conversation analysis on the dialogue. For example, use the conversation at the Getty Center between Tash and Aidan, the dinner conversation between Tash and Lu, the poolside conversation between Monroe and Tash, or one of the conversations between Lu and Paisley.

2. Conduct a content analysis of the art and popular culture referenced in the book.

3. Research the #MeToo Movement or Time's Up initiative. Conduct additional research to locate peer-reviewed articles or scholarly essays on the issues these movements address (sexual harassment, sexual assault, rape culture, gender pay and employment inequities), and then write a paper using the experiences of one or more of the characters in *Film* to illustrate or challenge your research.

ART ACTIVITIES

1. Create a visual or audio-visual version of *Pop Candy*, Tash's short film. You could use film or a visual arts media such as drawing, painting, or comics.

2. Respond artistically to *Film*. Using any media – literary, visual, or performative – create an artistic response to a theme in the novel or illustrate how the novel made you feel. Write a brief artist's statement to accompany the work.

3. Create a piece of art, in any media, that could be a part of the group show at Patty Price's gallery. Think about how the piece complements or relates to Tash's short film. Title the piece.

BLUE, CHAPTER 1

That can't be right, Tash thought, squinting again to look at the time. "Shit," she said as she reached for the alarm clock. "Damn thing never works," she mumbled while placing it back on her nightstand. *I'm gonna be late again. I should hurry.* She rolled over before slowly stretching her arms and lazily dragging herself out of bed. Stumbling to her dresser and opening the top drawer, she rifled around for underwear before heading to the bathroom.

Twenty minutes later, wrapped in a towel after showering, she used her palm to wipe the steam from the mirror. *I look like crap. God, I hope I can cover those bags under my eyes*, she thought as she started to apply her signature black liquid eyeliner. *I'll use gray eyeshadow and make them smoky.* Realizing it must be getting late, she dried and straightened her long, dirty-blonde hair but skipped curling the ends to save time. Returning to her bedroom, she scoured her closet wondering what to wear before deciding on an off-the-shoulder, loose white tunic, a pair of skinny black jeans, and high-heeled black leather booties. Staring at herself in the mirror, she tried on four pairs of earrings, posing left and then right to fully view each option, before deciding on gold hoops. To match, she threw on her favorite gold, turquoise, and red evil-eye bracelet. *Coffee. I need coffee.*

En route to the galley kitchen, Tash stomped past her roommates' closed bedroom doors, clomping her heels without concern as to whether they were asleep. She got a bag of coffee and the nearly empty carton of milk out of the refrigerator, placed them on the counter, and opened the cupboard to get a coffee filter and her to-go tumbler, neither of which were there. She found her tumbler in the sink, dirty from the day before. *Fuck.* Turning back to focus on the coffee pot, she spotted a note sitting beside it. *There's nothing I dread first thing in the freaking morning more than these notes.*

Morning, Tash. Hope you didn't forget to turn the volume up on your alarm again and oversleep. I didn't want to wake you in case you had the day off. We're out of coffee filters and it's your turn to go to the store. I left my list on the back of this note. I can't cover for you this time so please go. Thanks. Have a nice day. Penelope

Tash flipped over the note and rolled her eyes. She started to leave the kitchen when she turned back, remembering to put the milk away. *Don't want the Gestapo after me for that again*, she thought. She headed into the common room, sans coffee, and looked around. *Where did I leave my bag?* The small loveseat was overflowing with random clothing, topped with her black blazer. *Hmm. Two pairs of men's shoes under the coffee table. Jason must have met someone. Good for him, but where's my stupid bag? Ah, there you are*, spotting her black bag hiding in the corner, with her keys and sunglasses conveniently lying on top of it. She scooped them up, put her dark glasses on, and headed out, double locking the door behind her.

"Hi, Mr. Collier," she said, passing her neighbor on the stairs.

"Good morning, Miss," he replied.

Despite the morning rush, she was able to hail a cab quickly. As the cab passed Washington Square Park, she stared at the chess players, already at it for the day. Soon she drifted into thoughts of the drama the day before. *Ray was a jerk, Jason was so right. He didn't deserve me. I'm glad I ended it.* As they pulled up to Alice & Olivia, Tash rummaged through her bag for cash before giving up and surrendering her credit card to the driver.

She flew into the store, quickly heading to the backroom before Catherine could open her mouth. Tash threw her arm up and hollered, "I know, and I'm sorry. My alarm didn't go off and blah, blah, blah."

"You're half an hour late, again," Catherine called after her.

"I know, I know, and I'm sorry," Tash said, rolling her eyes. As she hung her bag and blazer on a coat hook, Catherine continued to reprimand her.

"You need to get a new alarm clock then, because I…"

"I'll close for you tonight, okay? You can leave early; it's fine."

"You know if you left on time you could walk here and save yourself the cab fare. You probably lose at least an hour's wages by creating a situation in which you need to take a cab. And is it even faster with the morning traffic?"

As Catherine continued, Tash muttered under her breath, "Get off my ass, you bitch," if only to make herself feel better. She took a deep breath and headed to the Keurig machine to make some much-needed coffee. She plugged it in and flipped the switch, but Catherine exclaimed, "Don't bother. It broke yesterday." Tash squeezed her eyes shut, shook her head, and took another deep breath before forcing a smile onto her face. "Great, that's just great."

***

"I'm going to head out now, since you're closing tonight."

"Uh huh, fine Catherine. Have a good night," Tash said while leaning on the store counter and checking her phone. She was exchanging texts with Jason, reminding him to get them on the club list that weekend.

"Make sure you change the shoes and handbags in the window display. Last season's accessories go on sale tomorrow, so the newer items should be featured in the window."

"Uh huh," Tash said, without looking up from her phone.

"Okay, well, goodnight."

"Night, Catherine."

An hour later, after ringing up the final customers, Tash retrieved the new handbags and shoes from the backroom. She liked working on window displays because it was a chance to be creative and put things together in unexpected ways that were sure to perplex Catherine. Tash imagined the windows as still images from film, designed to convey a feeling as much as to display clothes. While there was a limit to what she could get away with, she pushed the bounds as much as possible. She didn't mind her job and loved working in SoHo, but window displays and the employee discount were the only aspects from which she derived genuine pleasure.

Once Tash was done putting accessories from the window onto the sale table, she gathered her things and locked up. With only a blazer on, she felt a chill. These early spring days were unusually warm but the evenings were still cold. *I should really walk home. I can't blow more money on a cab.* Desperate for a scarf, she stood on Greene Street rummaging through her slouchy leather hobo bag, which she carried everywhere despite its tendency to become a black hole in which she couldn't find anything. "Ah, there we go," she whispered as she pulled out a periwinkle scarf, which she double wrapped around her neck.

As the sky darkened, the SoHo lights seemed to shine at their brightest. Store windows screamed with flashing light bulbs, a frenetic attempt to command notice. Tash looked in the windows as she passed by, tempted by sale signs even though she was accustomed to them. These days, even New York City itself was on sale. Street vendors yearning to end their days well tried to entice her with sunglasses and other trinkets. When she smiled and shook her head, one guy screamed, "You look like Lindsay Lohan. You're dope."

"I get that a lot," she said with a mischievous smile.

As she crossed over into the Village, the restaurants and corner cafés were already bustling with people clamoring to sit outside. After a brutal winter, New Yorkers were ready to enjoy outdoor dining again. Waiters turned on heat lamps and uncorked wine bottles amid casual conversation and bubbling laughter.

Her feet sore, she slowed her pace as she passed Washington Square Park. As day turned to night, the park was the center of the world around her. People from all walks of life appeared. The parade of artists, writers, students, homeless people, drug dealers, professors, tourists, and countless others made it the perfect microcosm of the city itself, the dream and its shadow side. She overheard a group of preppy college students talking about social justice as they passed Harold, actively trying not to notice as he set up his sleeping bag on a bench. *Jerks*, she thought. *They're such posers.*

A year earlier, Tash had twisted her ankle racing to work one morning. A barrage of f-bombs flew out of her mouth. Harold, a witness to the accident, helped her to a bench and told her not to curse.

"Are you for real?" she asked.

"It's undignified," he replied. "Do you think you can walk?"

"Uh, yeah, but not in these shoes."

They spoke for a few more minutes before she decided to stumble back to her apartment to ice her ankle and change shoes. Since that day, she'd say hi to Harold when she saw him and stopped to talk with him at least once every couple of weeks, usually bringing him a cup of coffee and sometimes a donut. Powdered sugar was his favorite.

He once started to tell his life story and she interrupted saying, "It's cool, Harold. We don't have to do this. I don't need you to explain." He seemed relieved. Since then, their conversations were usually about how they were each doing that particular day. Although routinely chased away by the police, he always returned. On this night, she just waved as she passed him.

Only half a block from her apartment, she had the horrible realization that she was supposed to get groceries. Not willing to endure a lecture from Penelope, she passed her apartment building and headed to the corner grocer. After grabbing a hand basket and making a beeline to the freezer for some ice cream, she started searching for Penelope's grocery list. As she fumbled for the list, mumbling, "Ah, where is that stupid thing?" she heard a voice say, "Maybe you'd have better luck if you shut your eyes and put your hand in."

"Huh?" she queried, looking up at the six-foot-tall guy standing before her, dressed from head to toe in black. He had bleached blonde spiky hair, high cheekbones, a strong jawline, and a piercing through his right eyebrow that she thought was simultaneously cool and disgusting.

"You know, sometimes if you're looking too hard, you can't find anything."

"Uh, yeah," she said, staring into his evergreen eyes. *Oh my God, he's seriously hot.*

"Here, tell me what you're looking for and I'll shut my eyes and stick my hand in for you."

Raising her eyebrows, she said, "How stupid do you think I am? Maybe I should just go outside and scream, 'Somebody rob me!'"

He laughed. "Fair enough, but you try it."

Tash smirked and stuck her hand into her bag without looking. "Uh huh, here it is!" she exclaimed as she pulled out the small, crumpled paper. "That's uncanny."

"Sometimes you just have to concentrate less, you know?" he said. "What's so important, anyway?"

"Oh, it's just my roommate's grocery list. She's pretty uptight so I can't screw it up. You wouldn't believe the things she writes, like 'two organic red apples and flax seed powder,' whatever the hell that is. Anyway, I should probably get back to shopping."

He smiled and waved his arm, to indicate she could pass by. With only a few aisles in the small store, Tash bumped into him again in the produce section.

"Should I even ask what that's about?" she said while giggling, looking at the twenty or more coconuts in his basket.

"Oh, these are for a party I'm deejaying for a couple of friends over at NYU."

"They're serving whole coconuts?" she asked, mystified.

He laughed. "People try to get them open. It's like a drinking game kind of thing. It's pretty funny."

"Gotcha. Do you go to NYU?"

"No, I went to school in Chicago and moved to New York after I graduated. I'm a professional deejay. I'm just doing this party as a favor."

"So, what kinds of clubs do you spin at?" she asked.

"Uh, well, tomorrow I'll be spinning at the Forever 21 store in Times Square."

She smiled. "Well, do you get a discount at least?"

He laughed. "Didn't think to ask for that. So, what's your name?"

"Natashya, but my friends call me Tash."

"I'm Aidan. Do you live around here?"

"Just a block away. I share a place with two roommates."

"Pretty awesome area to live in, good for you."

"Yeah, well we're in like the only non-restored building in the neighborhood. Don't get me wrong, I love living here and it's pretty close to my work, but we're not in one of the swanky buildings with a marble entrance. It's more like splintery wood floors and a scary old-fashioned elevator that makes me want to take the stairs."

He smiled. "What's your work?"

"I work at a couple of stores in SoHo."

"For the discount, right?" he said with a smirk.

Tash laughed. "Well, nice to meet you but I've gotta finish up and get going."

"Sure, me too. Maybe I'll see you around. If you're not busy, stop by Forever 21 tomorrow."

"I have to work."

"Well, can I maybe get your number?" he asked.

"Why don't you give me yours instead?"

"Sure, that's cool." He put his coconut-filled basket on the ground and held out his hand. "Give me your phone and I'll put it in."

"You don't want me to have to search my bag again. Here," she said, handing him the note with Penelope's grocery list. "Do you have a pen?"

Aidan smiled and pulled a red crayon out of his pocket. "Don't ask," he said as he wrote his number on the little paper. "Here," he said handing it to her. "See ya."

"See ya," she said.

When she casually glanced around the store a few minutes later, he was gone. She brought her basket to the checkout. The cashier asked, "Did you find everything you needed?"

"Yeah, yeah I did."

***

Her feet aching and her arms overloaded, Tash felt like she was going to drop by the time she made it home. She dumped her handbag and keys on the entryway floor and swung the shopping bags onto the kitchen counter. She opened her new box of popcorn and stuck a packet in the microwave before putting the rest of the groceries away. She giggled to herself, thinking about the coconuts filling Aidan's basket. *I wonder if Jason is home.*

Tash met Jason Woo at a club a few years earlier. She was having trouble getting past the bouncers when Jason came to her rescue. His modeling career was just starting to take off thanks to landing a gig as Calvin Klein's first Asian male model. Both sarcastic and carefree, they bonded immediately and moved in together as soon as Tash graduated from college. Though they had a hard time looking out for themselves, they did a remarkable job of looking out for each other.

Tash was so lost in thought about Aidan's coconuts that she didn't hear Jason approaching.

"Hey," Jason said from the doorway.

"Oh, hey." She tossed him a bag of coffee. "Stick that in the fridge." As he put the coffee away, Tash said, "This too," and flung the loaf of bread.

"I can't believe you actually went shopping. Did Pen leave you one of her famous notes?"

"Yup," she said just when the microwave beeped. "Is she in her room studying?"

"She's not here. I think she had dinner plans with her study group or something."

"Seriously? She's unbelievable, making me do all this when she's not even here," she said as she opened the popcorn bag. Steam burned her hand and caused her to drop the bag on the counter. "Fuck," she mumbled.

"How is it you never learn not to open it that way?" Jason asked facetiously. "Here, I got it," he said. He grabbed a bowl from the cupboard and emptied the bag for her.

"You know if you leave it in the bag it's one less dish to wash. That's why I do that."

"Since when do you ever wash the dishes anyway?" he rebuffed, as he ate a handful of her popcorn.

"I don't know why she made me go to the store if she wasn't even gonna be home," Tash said as she threw the two empty grocery bags in the garbage.

"I know you can't relate, but some people actually plan ahead. She probably wanted breakfast."

"Oh, right, like you plan ahead," Tash jabbed, tossing a jar of maraschino cherries.

"You're lucky I caught that. What is it with you and these things?" he asked, sticking them in the door of the refrigerator.

"You know I love them. I can't help it," she said. "But listen, I kind of met a guy. I met him at the store while I was getting Pen's crap, so maybe it was meant to be."

"You met a guy? Ah, do tell," he prodded.

"Well from the looks of things this morning, I'm guessing you also met a guy, so you tell first." She opened the refrigerator and grabbed two cans of Diet Coke.

"Some lighting guy from the shoot. I kicked him out this morning."

"You're such a slut. Must be hard to be so irresistible," Tash bemused.

Jason smiled. "You would know. Come on, let's go curl up on my bed and you can tell me all about the guy you met. I hope he's better than Ray. I'm eating half this popcorn, by the way," he said, taking a fistful and heading to his room.

"Hey, that's my dinner!"

ACKNOWLEDGEMENTS

Thank you to everyone at Brill | Sense for supporting this book and my growth as an author. Special thanks to John Bennett, Marti Huetink, Peter de Liefde, Paul Chambers, Jolanda Karada, Evelien van der Veer, and Robert van Gameren. Thank you to the editorial advisory board members of the *Social Fictions* series for your generosity and to the early reviewers for your kind endorsements. Heartfelt thanks to Shalen Lowell, the world's best assistant, spiritual bodyguard, and friend. Thank you to Clear Voice Editing for the phenomenal copyediting services. Tori Amos, "I found out where my edge is." Thanks for the musical guidance and inspirational chats along the way. To my social media community and colleagues, thank you boundlessly for your support. My deepest gratitude to my friends and family, especially Tony Adams, Vanessa Alssid, Melissa Anyiwo, Pamela DeSantis, Sandra Faulkner, Ally Field, Robert Charles Gompers, Laurel Richardson, Mr. Barry Mark Shuman, Jessica Smartt Gullion, and Adrienne Trier-Bieniek. Celine Boyle, thank you for your comments and edits during the writing process and for making it so much fun. You are the writing buddy I dreamed of as a kid. Madeline Leavy-Rosen, you are my light. I love you always. Mark Robins, you're the best spouse in the world. Thank you for getting who I am, supporting my creativity, and helping me to become the best version of myself. I love you always, too. To all those who haunt these pages, I remember you. I dedicate this book to everyone who has stumbled while pursuing a dream but found the courage to keep going, and to those who have lent a helping hand.

ABOUT THE AUTHOR

Patricia Leavy, Ph.D., is an independent scholar and bestselling author. She was formerly Associate Professor of Sociology, Chair of Sociology & Criminology, and Founding Director of Gender Studies at Stonehill College in Massachusetts. She has published over twenty-five books, earning commercial and critical success in both nonfiction and fiction, and her work has been translated into numerous languages. Her recent titles include *Handbook of Arts-Based Research; Research Design: Quantitative, Qualitative, Mixed Methods, Arts-Based, and Community-Based Participatory Research Approaches; Method Meets Art: Arts-Based Research Practice, Second Edition; Fiction as Research Practice; The Oxford Handbook of Qualitative Research*; and the novels *Spark, Blue, American Circumstance,* and *Low-Fat Love*. She is also series creator and editor for eight book series with Oxford University Press and Brill | Sense, and is co-founder and co-editor-in-chief of *Art/Research International: A Transdisciplinary Journal*. A vocal advocate of public scholarship, she blogs for *The Huffington Post, The Creativity Post, Mogul*, and *We Are the Real Deal*, and is frequently called on by the US news media. In addition to receiving numerous accolades for her books, she has received career awards from the New England Sociological Association, the American Creativity Association, the American Educational Research Association, the International Congress of Qualitative Inquiry, and the National Art Education Association. In 2016, Mogul, a global women's empowerment network, named her an "Influencer." In 2018, she was honored by the National Women's Hall of Fame, and State University of New York at New Paltz established the "Patricia Leavy Award for Art and Social Justice." Please visit www.patricialeavy.com for more information and links to her social media.

Printed in the United States
By Bookmasters